Working with Consultants

*How to Become a More Effective
Client and Maximize the Value from
Consulting Projects*

Peter Wuensche

Zeno Publications

Zeno Pulbications
1 Cornwall Mews West
London SW7 4BH
United Kingdom

www.zenopublications.com
info@zenopublications.com

Published in the United Kingdom in 2013 by Zeno Publications

A catalogue record of this book is available from the British Library.

ISBN: 978-0-9572845-0-0

Contents

Introduction

When I suggest to people that most consulting clients are not very good at working with consultants, they generally either agree with me or blame the consultants. So I should start by saying that I shall not be playing the blame game in this book.

This is not because I disagree with those who criticise consultants—in my twenty years as a consultant I have seen plenty of examples of poor practice—but because I don't think the issue can be effectively addressed on the consultant side of the equation. This has, of course, been tried: books criticising or 'exposing' consultants already exist (as do countless press articles and even TV programmes); attempts have been made to establish a professional body to monitor standards and police the industry; there has even been talk of regulation. But how can anyone hope to impose standards on an industry as diverse and fragmented as consulting? Rules that apply equally to a university researcher who provides specialised consulting on his area of expertise and a global consulting firm that employs thousands of people have to be so general as to be meaningless.

On the other hand, I do firmly believe that individual client organizations can do much to raise their game and, by extension, that of the consultants they work with. If enough clients do this, perhaps the overall quality of consulting will improve too.

I became convinced that significant value was being lost on both sides of the client-consultant relationship quite early in my career. The issue has continued to preoccupy me and I have often discussed it with clients and with other consultants. Most of these conversations have gravitated around four questions:

- Does it matter whether clients are good at working with consultants?
- What does it mean to be 'good' at using consultants?
- Why aren't clients better at it?
- What can clients do to build this capability?

The main aim of this book is to address the last of these questions—to provide a practical, coherent and structured approach to improving the way an organization uses consultants. But to put this in context, I will start by taking a look at the other three questions.

Does it matter?

It is easy to dismiss consulting as an irrelevance—a peripheral factor in the business environment which has little or no impact on an organization's success. For most managers, the way their organization relates to consultants is an afterthought, occasionally brought up as part of a project review, but even then well down the priority list.

It is also argued that, as the consulting industry has developed, many of the most obvious failings have been addressed—that what we have now, though imperfect, is 'good enough' and improving it further would require far too much effort to be worthwhile.

There is some truth in both of these views, but a number of factors have conspired to make them less relevant today:

Firstly, the growth of the consulting industry has made consultants increasingly difficult for managers to ignore. Very few organizations of any size manage to avoid using consultants altogether and large organizations can spend hundreds of millions of dollars on consultants in any given year. This is often a significant proportion of controllable costs and it behoves managers to ensure that this money is well spent.

This imperative has been reinforced by the relentless drive for ever greater productivity, increasingly in the public sector as well as the private. Where the cost/benefit ratio of using consultants may have seemed satisfactory in the past, it often seems less so now when it is compared with the gains to be had in other areas.

At the same time, the drive for efficiency (both at the operational and the strategic levels) has led to a greater need to focus an organization's skills and resources, to understand what the organization needs to be good at and develop this while reducing costs in other areas. It is no longer possible to be good (or even adequate) in each activity in the value chain and it has become a rare luxury to be able to throw resources at problems and initiatives which, however important, are not core to the organization's long-term portfolio of activities. And even when you can afford this luxury, increasing specialization means that the people who are available internally may not have the right skills to accomplish such tasks effectively.

These trends are accentuated by factors such as the increasing role of technology, regulation, internationalization and an ever more uncertain and volatile geopolitical environment.

The net result of all this is that the traditional model of the organization as a self-sufficient 'production engine' is becoming more nuanced and value is increasingly sought outside the organization as much as within it. This can be seen in the fragmentation and reconfiguration of manufacturing supply chains and in the increasing use of outsourced services. These developments have long since passed the stage where they are simply efficiency improvements (if they ever really were): they are strategic moves which fundamentally alter organizational strategy, design and business models.

These changes have significant implications both for the role of consultants and for the ways organizations use them. Because a more open model of the organization requires greater flexibility than the traditional model (and vice versa), these organizations are relying less on traditional employment contracts and more on bought-in services—employees, especially in the service sector, are becoming contractors or consultants (albeit in the broadest sense of the term). And some of them at least have welcomed this change: in some areas of IT, for instance, it is often difficult to hire staff on a permanent basis because most prefer to work as independent contractors or small teams of consultants.

If such trends continue, it means that the consulting industry is set to grow substantially and will come to represent a larger proportion of an organization's budget, while the range of services consultants offer will continue to broaden.

For most organizations, consultants, contractors and other external service providers are already a fact of life (indeed, not using them would be to deny the organization one of the main weapons in its resourcing armoury). Yet the ways in which these relationships are managed remain highly transactional. They are an afterthought—a useful, flexible resource which can be drawn upon when internal resources are insufficient. Although this function of consultants will remain valuable, it falls well short of harnessing the value that consultants can offer an organization. If the role of consultants continues to develop in the ways I have described above, an organization's ability to manage them could well develop from a hygiene factor into a strategic lever, perhaps even a competitive strength.

What is 'good' use of consultants?

This may seem like an academic question. It isn't: it is all very well for someone to say that they want to improve how their organization works with consultants, but what precisely are they going to improve? Where do they think this will take them? How will they know if they are making progress or not?

In a very general sense, good use of consultants is, quite simply, that which delivers the most value to the client organization. But the factors that affect this value will vary from one organization to another: for one client it may be critical to be able to access specialist consulting expertise quickly; another might need to co-ordinate multiple consultants on the same project; yet another may find that the greatest value comes from the knowledge that is passed from the consultants to the internal team and will focus on facilitating this process. Different factors may also be more relevant for one consultant than another: it would make no sense, for instance, to assess your ability to work with a consultant engaged to implement an IT system on the same basis as your ability to work with a brand specialist.

The list of factors to consider is potentially endless, but it is essential that clients should try to understand which factors drive value for them, how this will affect their consulting choices and, consequently, which consulting-related capabilities they need to develop internally.

When I speak to people about how their organizations assess their use of consultants, almost all of them think in terms of projects or contracts. Often opinions are based on the success or failure of specific, high profile projects. Success is defined as meeting or exceeding the objectives set out in the original consulting brief.

From this perspective, an organization would be good at using consultants if the majority of the projects which it undertook were judged to be successful.

But when you look at it in a broader context, the problems with this approach start to emerge. An organization might have a 100% success rate on its consulting projects, but could still be making poor use of consultants because it has not taken adequate account of how, where and why these consultants have been used. For instance, the projects' objectives may not be correctly aligned with the organization's goals; or they may be out of date by the time the project is completed; or again, the wrong choice of consultant may have been made, resulting in suboptimal results or costs which are unnecessarily high. These are just a few examples of cases where, although the projects may be considered successful, the organization's use of consultants is not as good as it could be. Conversely, at the project level things may not be going so well, but this may not be because of the way the client is using its consultants—in fact, this may be the only thing that is preventing the situation from getting much worse.

The other common yardstick by which some organizations assess their use of consultants is cost. This measure is particularly favoured by those who consider consultants a 'necessary evil' and consequently judge the organization's effectiveness in managing consultants by how little they are used. It should be clear from the preceding pages that I disagree with this approach and I do not intend to discuss it here. But I should point out that, even in this view, the costs of using consultants are commonly underestimated, once again because of an overly narrow focus. In particular, the costs of internal resources and of disruption to the organization are rarely taken into account.

Finally, and in my view most importantly, a broader assessment of an organization's use of consultants should take into account its ability to work alongside consultants and to extract the value from the work which the consultants do across the consulting relationships. The achievement of these goals is dependent on a set of skills, competencies, processes and structures which few, if any, organizations take the time to develop.

Why aren't clients better at working with consultants?

The inability to make effective use of consultants can be ascribed to four main factors: a perception that consulting is unimportant to the organization, reluctance among senior managers to take the lead in sorting out how the organization uses consultants, a highly transactional approach to the way consultants are managed, and outright hostility to consultants in general.

'It's not important'

There is often a perception among clients that consulting is peripheral to their organization's activities. This may well be true if one looks at it from a budgetary perspective (consulting spend, even when it is high, is likely to be a relatively small proportion of an organization's overall cost base), but, as I described earlier, consultants and other service suppliers are an increasingly important factor in how organizations work, so much so that they are becoming a consideration in organizational design.

Ultimately, though, measures of activity, whether relative or absolute, will not help you get a handle on the importance of consultants to your organization because this is a function of the output of consultants' work rather than the inputs. Consulting activities are often concerned with the fabric of the organization—its strategy, structure, processes and activities. This means that the impact they have on an organization, for better or worse, is often out of all proportion to the effort or cost involved.

'It's not my job'

It is rare to find anyone prepared to take the lead in sorting out how an organization relates to and uses consultants. This is hardly surprising—if consulting is not perceived as an issue, managers see no reason to add to their already high workload by taking responsibility for it. And even if someone could make the time, there is little in it for them: sales, deals, making acquisitions or disposals or cutting costs all lead to glory and financial rewards. The person who sorts out consulting is unlikely to get more than a pat on the back.

A consequence of this lack of leadership is that the relationship competencies which are needed to use consultants effectively are never developed or applied. The very factors which are leading to an increase in the use of consultants—organizational streamlining and focus on core competencies—are preventing the development of new competencies for managing consultants.

The absence of this framework of competencies puts huge pressure on managers who have to deal with consultants. They try to muddle through with a combination of purchasing 'best practice' and generic project management disciplines, but often find themselves struggling because they do not have, and cannot access, the other skills and resources that are needed. This in turn makes them even less inclined to take responsibility for an issue that they do not feel qualified to deal with.

'They should do the project and get out'

The role of consultants has changed considerably over the years. Clients' perceptions of this role have not: the generally held view seems to be that consultants are brought in to obtain specific information, deliver discrete projects or provide formal advice in their area of expertise. The organization interacts with consultants by setting the terms of reference and accepting (or not) the deliverables at the end of the project. In this view, consultants differ from contractors in that contractors are managed by the client whereas consultants manage their own projects in accordance with the agreed terms of reference.

This view has the virtue of being neat and tidy, but the considerable disadvantage of not tallying with the facts on the ground: consulting projects rarely fit into neat, discrete packages. They tend to change shape and size over time as circumstances change and requirements are altered and there are often many links between one piece of consulting work and others. A consulting project is nearly always a collaborative undertaking, requiring at least as much input from the client organization as it does from the consultants. And the distinctions between consultants and contractors are blurred at best and are increasingly becoming meaningless.

'We don't need consultants'

Consultants can trigger strong reactions among the client's employees, at all levels of the organization. Some feel insecure because they think they should be doing the job the consultants have been brought in to do or because they are afraid that the outcome of the consulting project will be them losing their job. Others may have experience of senior management 'vanity projects' and tar all consulting projects with the same brush. Or again, there may be rancour because someone's pet project was considered lower priority than a consulting project. I have worked with clients whose experience of a single, disastrous consulting project has made the entire organization (except the new CEO) extremely hostile.

Taken together, the these four inhibiting factors contribute to an environment of failure (or at least under-performance) in the interactions the client organization has with consultants. In some organizations, managers who are given the task of leading a consulting project see it as a 'poisoned chalice' and spend as much of their time trying to mitigate the political damage of failure as they do trying to achieve success.

If the situation is bad at the managerial level, it is generally worse lower down the organizational hierarchy. As nobody wants to take a lead on how the organization interacts with consultants, employees are left to define the form of this interaction based on their own priorities, prejudices and interpretation of what the company wants to achieve. And this rather chaotic state of affairs is thrown into further confusion by periodic directives which may come down from above.

What can be done about it?

Given the context described above, it is perhaps not surprising that few managers are inclined to take on the task of sorting out how their organization uses consultants. For those who are willing to rise to the challenge, this book provides a framework and some of the tools you will need, whether your goal is modest (to improve the value for money you get from the consultants you use) or ambitious (turning consultants into a strategic asset for the organization, providing flexibility and greatly extending its capabilities).

Who should read this book?

Books about consulting tend to fall into one of three categories: memoirs, biographies and exposés by consultants which are usually either highly complimentary or highly critical of the industry;

books about how to become a consultant (and get rich doing it); and manuals for managers who need to run consulting projects.

This book falls primarily into the third of these categories (with a few elements of the first), but with some important differences: there seemed little point in simply repeating what others have already covered quite adequately and much of the material contained in such volumes is omitted here. The focus is on the (relatively) advanced use of consultants—how you need to set up your organization when you know that you will be using consultants regularly and want to get as much out of them as possible. It is aimed at readers who are not satisfied with the value that their organization is getting from its consultants and want to do something about it.

Consequently, the readers who will find this book most useful will be managers in organizations that are 'heavy users' of consulting. This not only includes those that spend a lot of money on consulting, but also those for whom an ability to work with consultants can be seen as materially affecting performance. Some of the approaches I put forward go to the heart of how organizations work and, in view of these organizational design implications, they will be of use to board level management and strategists, as well as to executives who have to deal with more practical, operational issues.

Although heavy users of consulting are the main target, there is plenty here for the lighter user and for those who have a less direct interest in consultants. The first three chapters are a primer on the consulting industry and should be useful for anyone who wants to gain a better understanding of how consultants work, from the student looking at a career in consulting right up to the experienced executive. And the approach described in the subsequent chapters is, I hope, sufficiently adaptable to bring some measure of benefit to anyone who works with consultants. For many organizations, consulting is primarily a resourcing issue and so the material here should also be of interest to all those involved in resolving the resourcing conundrum. In particular, I have noticed that many recruitment consultants have broadened their scope from permanent hires to interims and contractors and now even consultants. While they may be less relevant as a source of business to the larger consulting firms, they can play a very useful role as an intermediary between smaller consultants and their clients.

Lastly, this book is not intended as a cudgel for clients to beat up their consultants. Where I could, I have tried to focus on opportunities to benefit both parties in the relationship. So I hope that some of these ideas will be of interest to consultants too and that they will help them develop and improve their relationships with their clients.

How to use this book

The ideas presented here are not based on academic research nor are they theoretical. They are based on practical experience and on many discussions with consultants and their clients who have had to deal with the issues discussed. In view of these origins, I have started by looking at ways of addressing some of these practical issues and only later addressed the potential strategic opportunities and implications.

The book and the approach it describes are modular—each element of the approach can be taken independently. But I have also included a framework of suggestions and guidelines that should help you combine these elements to create your own approach.

I have tried to avoid being prescriptive, partly because I dislike the facile, simplistic nature of much business literature and partly because the nature of the problem precludes a prescriptive approach—there are simply too many possible scenarios. This lack of prescription necessarily makes some of the book a little more complex because I try to present options and ways to choose between them rather than ready-made solutions. But the advantage of this is that these suggestions should be easier to implement because you will have tackled key issues and made the necessary choices before you start implementation. And implementation matters: this book will benefit you far more if you take a single idea from a single chapter and do it, than if you read the whole book a hundred times and implement nothing.

In view of this, I have tried to structure the book to be as flexible as possible. It can be read all the way through or you can pick out the bits which are relevant to you and your organization. Some sections contain material which will be familiar to many. For instance, if you have been a consultant, you may wish to skip the first three chapters in which I look at how consultants work. In the same vein, there are many areas covered here in which I am far less expert than others. If you happen to be an expert on, say, training or relationship management, you will probably not learn much on that subject from this book beyond a few pointers on how it can be applied to consultants.

The sequence in which you read the chapters can also be varied to suit your requirements: if you are taking a strategic view, you may want to start with the final chapter and then work back through the earlier material depending on how it fits with your strategic thinking; on the other hand, if you are looking to cut consulting costs and improve efficiency, you will probably find the sections on the consulting process, benefits quantification and portfolio management more helpful.

Within each chapter there is a mix of material: some is more conceptual in nature and is aimed at clients who are trying to work out what their approach to consulting should be; some is more practical and is aimed at those who have already specified a set of goals and are looking for help in achieving them. I appreciate that not everybody will be interested in both and I have tried to place signposts in the text to help readers pick out the bits that are of interest to them.

Lastly, for readers who would like to explore these matters further, you can look on my publisher's website, www.zenopublications.com, for links to my website and blog. I welcome feedback and (to the extent that time permits) I would be happy to discuss any questions you may have about the book or other consulting matters.

Where do I find the bit about ...?

The first three chapters are intended to help readers get a better understanding of how consultants work. Rather than trying to cover all areas, I have focused on those aspects which I feel are important but frequently overlooked.

Chapter 1 examines the consulting business model—how consulting firms work as businesses. This includes cost structures, key value drivers, sales approaches and pricing. The business model drives consultant behaviour, including many of the behaviours which clients find puzzling or annoying.

Chapter 2 is intended to help people who have difficulty finding their way through the huge variety of consultant offerings on the market. It looks at the factors which differentiate consultants with an emphasis on the intangibles that are rarely considered during consultant selection processes.

Chapter 3 is about the consulting process—the set of steps which are common to most consulting projects. I look at each step in the process and where (in my experience) each step commonly goes wrong.

While the first three chapters focus mainly on consultants, the remaining chapters take a closer look at the client organization and how it interacts with the consultants it uses.

Chapter 4 starts by suggesting ways to assess what is to be gained by improving how you work with consultants and goes on to set out the four key building blocks of my overall approach—the 'consulting mix'.

Chapter 5 looks at what you need to know about consultants and consulting. It introduces the concept of knowledge management, examines how this can be applied to consulting and gives some pointers on how to assemble a consulting 'knowledge base'.

Chapter 6 continues the knowledge management theme, but with a focus on how your organization can learn to work more effectively with consultants and suggests ways of building your organization's capabilities in this area through procedures, the sharing of experience and training.

Chapter 7 describes the advantages of taking a portfolio approach to managing consultants and consulting projects as opposed to managing each in isolation. It goes on to look at how such an approach can be implemented.

Chapter 8 is about building and maintaining the relationships between an organization and the consulting firms it uses.

Chapter 9 provides some guidelines for putting the different elements described in the previous chapters into a coherent consulting strategy that is appropriate for your organization.

Finally, *Chapter 10* takes a more strategic view, examining the implications of taking these suggestions to their logical conclusion and placing consultants in the context of broader organizational design and development opportunities.

CHAPTER 1

The Consulting Business Model

When working with any supplier, it is generally advisable to have a good understanding of their business model—how they make money. This is most obvious at the negotiation of the supply contract, but is of equal importance for subsequent conflict avoidance, problem-solving and general relationship management. This is not just good business practice, but plain common sense.

It may come as some surprise then that, in 20 years of consulting, I have never once been asked by a client to explain my business to them. And even when I have offered to explain it, my offer has only been taken up on a couple of occasions. There are, I think, three main reasons for this:

- They don't want to know
- They believe the focus should be on the relationship
- They already know (or think they know)

Clients can have various reasons for not wanting to know: they may think it unimportant or perhaps they simply have no time. If you are in the latter camp, all I can say to you is that it is a relatively small investment of time that usually pays back over the course of a single project and brings substantial value if you are in a long-term relationship.

For those who feel that if there is a strong relationship, everything else will fall into place, my advice is 'it won't'. The quality of a relationship should not be allowed to obscure the fact that consulting is a business and is driven by business motives. You ignore these at your peril.

For those who feel that they already have a good grasp of what makes consultants tick, there are two points I would like to make.

Firstly, most clients (and some consultants) actually know far less about consulting than they think they do. This is fairly obvious from some of the things one hears them say and, more importantly, in their behaviours. This is particularly true with regard to consulting fees—many managers do not seem to understand that the cost structure of a consulting firm is not the same as their own and that a consulting 'resource' is likely to be more expensive. I am not saying that consultants never overcharge, but I would suggest that this practice is far less prevalent than some clients think. I have lost count of the number of times a client has chosen to run a project internally on the grounds that using consultants would be too expensive, only to find that the final cost ends up far greater than what they would have paid the consultant—and that's without counting the cost of bringing in a consultant to get the project back on track.

Secondly, even those clients who do have a good understanding of consulting—such as former consultants—would benefit from a clearer understanding of how a particular supplier works. The consulting business model may be relatively simple, but the variations between firms, however small, can make all the difference in the way the relationship works.

My advice to anyone planning on hiring a firm of consultants is to spend an hour asking about their business. It is true that not all consultants are forthcoming about how their business works and, clearly, consulting firms need to maintain secrecy with regard to certain sensitive client information, but there is little need to extend this to their own business (in which there is very little worth hiding). So, if the consultants you are talking to do not want to tell you about their business, be suspicious.

To understand the business model of a particular consultant or consulting firm, it helps to have some idea of what the key elements are so you can ask the right questions. The remainder of this chapter sets out what I think a client ought to know about the generic consulting business model and some of the variations you are most likely to encounter, along with some suggestions about what to look out for when talking to a prospective supplier.

Cost structure

The essence of the consulting business model is really very simple (and perhaps this is why many clients think they already understand it): costs are made up mainly of salaries (80%-90%). The remainder are marketing costs, premises costs, IT, training, general overheads such as insurance, non-billable travel and bought-in research. These costs are covered by the fees earned from the client.

Although the cost components are likely to be the same for most consultancies, the relative weight of each component can vary considerably. For instance, some consulting firms place more emphasis on the quality of their recruitment (which is reflected in salaries) while others are less selective but have more robust training programmes; and some consulting firms will have a dedicated research department. All of these weightings will affect the price the firm charges, the charging mechanism and, to some extent, the types of work that they undertake.

Utilization—the key business driver

The key business driver in almost every consulting firm is not the price at which projects are sold or the number of projects, but 'utilization'. This is the proportion of available (and paid-for) consultant hours which are actually billed to the client. Given the choice between a project in which a large number of consultants are 'on the clock' (i.e. billing their time) for a long period of time at relatively low rates and a project employing few consultants for a short time at very high fee rates, most firms would choose the former. This is particularly true of IT consulting firms which tend to have legions of (relatively) low paid junior consultants. Junior consultants are very profitable for the firm when they are billing work, but, because of their numbers, very costly when they are not.

The other factors that affect utilization are: the relationship between the hours consultants actually work and what they are paid and charge for; the level of specialization of the consultants in the firm (generally speaking, the more flexible they are, the higher the average utilization); and the extent to which the firm invests in non-billable activities such as research and training and, most importantly, sales.

Sales and selling

After operating, selling is what most consultants spend most of their time doing. Some, especially at the senior levels, spend far more time on sales than they do actually consulting. Not surprisingly, the effectiveness of the sales process is the biggest factor in driving up a firm's utilization and consequently its profitability. This is because of the way consulting sales work. Like many industries involving high-value products or services, consulting tends to be a feast-or-famine business with very high sales costs. A consulting project will often take anywhere between two and twenty man weeks to sell. This equates to between $10 000 and $80 000 in salary costs alone. The sales cost is not directly related to the size of the project, although for very large projects it will tend to be higher. So selling multiple small projects quickly becomes uneconomical.

The exception to the above rule are so-called 'on-sales'. This term designates additional pieces of work sold to existing clients. Again, as in most other industries, it is much easier and less expensive to sell to existing clients than it is to sell to new ones. In consulting this is particularly true because a consulting team *in situ* is ideally positioned to identify, assess and raise issues which the client organization needs to address, and because on-sales do not involve the getting-to-know-you stages of new sales.

The drive to sell-on can be pushed to extremes: in one consulting firm, each member of the consulting team was required to fill out a form describing in some detail at least three opportunities for additional work—on the first day of the project!

This hard-nosed approach to selling consultancy is not always in the client's best interest: it distracts the consultants from the work in hand and it means that the issues which are later presented to the client are the ones which the consultants think they are most likely to sell rather than the ones which are most important for the client to resolve. The best way for the client to mitigate this, apart from strong relationship management, is to get in there first by scheduling feedback sessions in which the consultants are encouraged to give their views on the organization. This creates a forum to hear potentially valuable insights whilst ensuring that the client has enough control to prevent any undesirable pre-screening.

The aspect of consulting sales that I have heard most complaints about is when the client meets a number of senior consultants at the contracting stage of the project, only to find that these senior consultants disappear once the project is under way and are replaced by a much more junior team. I have even heard phrases like 'bait and switch' and 'con job' used in reference to this practice.

It is important for clients to be realistic here: a consultancy of any size in which senior consultants did not spend most of their time on sales and relationship management would swiftly go out of business. It would be like expecting board directors in a manufacturing company to spend the bulk of their time on the production line. The role of senior consultants is to maintain the client relationships, sell projects, ensure that appropriate resources are available and properly briefed for the projects to be delivered and oversee the quality of the work. They will typically have several projects under their control at any one time.

If you reset your expectations with this in mind, it becomes clear that the issue is not that you do not get the senior team, but that you do not always know in advance what team you do get. But, as I shall discuss in the next chapter, this is something you can control.

There may be times when you feel that the direct involvement of very senior consultants in an operating role is essential to the success of a project. If this is the case, you should raise the matter explicitly when scoping the work. Some sort of accommodation is usually achievable provided that you are flexible, prepared to pay and do not expect a 100% time commitment.

Pricing and charging mechanisms

Pricing is also largely driven by utilization (whatever consultants may tell you about value etc.). Standard pricing is usually calibrated so that the firm can break-even at about 40%-50% average utilization. Actual utilization is generally around 60% in an average year (based on the half dozen consulting firms of which I have direct experience). Pricing will vary somewhat depending on the cost structure: firms which undertake significant amounts of research or other activities which involve non-consulting staff will need to charge more for their consultants than firms which do not.

The cost structure is translated into a pricing scheme (usually in the form of 'Internal Billing Rates') which is communicated to the client through a charging mechanism. There are four basic mechanisms employed: fixed price projects, success fees, hourly/daily rates and value pricing.

Fixed-price contracts

Consultants dislike fixed-price projects for two reasons: firstly, they tend to be the ones where clients negotiate most on price and so there is little or no contingency if the scope needs to be changed or if the project runs into difficulties; and secondly, because of the lack of contingency, such projects can and often do lead to conflict between the consultants and the client over changes to scope. I have been on projects where the most senior people spent most of their time horse-trading about changes to the scope and deliverables.

For the client, a fixed price agreed in advance does offer the advantages of a reasonable level of certainty as to cost and sometimes a lower overall cost. The cost advantage is greater than it may at first appear because consultants are reasonably flexible when it comes to changes of scope and will allow a certain amount of 'scope creep' before they start looking to their contract. Too much of this, though, will lead to the conflicts mentioned above, which are no more to the client's advantage than they are to the consultant's. Fixed price projects work best when there is a relatively low level of uncertainty, when the scope of the work is unlikely to change and when it is easy to specify clearly what needs to be done for the work to be completed.

Success fees

Success-fee pricing would be even less popular with consultants than fixed price projects if consultants actually did work on a pure success fee basis. In most cases where consultants accept to work for success fees, they are 'bonuses' which have been negotiated on top of a regular fee rate (which at least covers the consultants' costs). Most consultants' business models are not structured to accommodate success-fee charging in its pure form. For it to work, consultants would have to charge similar rates to those charged by investment banks—I think many clients would feel that they were giving away too much value under this sort of arrangement.

For consultants, there are four further problems which have to be dealt with if this mechanism is to be effective. Firstly, there is the problem of defining and measuring what 'success' means. This problem can usually be overcome, but not without considerable time, effort and cost. Secondly, where longer projects are envisaged or where the results do not immediately become apparent, there is considerable cash flow risk for the consultants who do not normally need to maintain large reserves of working capital. Thirdly, consultants are not venture capitalists or investment bankers and may lack the skills to assess the risks involved and to equate them to an appropriate return. Even firms that offer investment advice as part of their service portfolio rarely apply these disciplines to their own projects with anything like the rigour that they would use for a client—the work required in structuring the success-fee charging mechanism can often exceed the fees to be earned. Lastly, and most importantly, consultants are rarely the determining factor in the success or failure of a project because it is the client who takes the decisions.

For clients, at first glance, success-fee charging has significant advantages: the cash outflow comes at the end of the project and is linked to real benefits; the consultant has 'skin in the game' and so is much more motivated to deliver value which, if the mechanism is correctly structured, can be substantially in excess of the value initially envisaged; and the consultant shares the risk with the client, often disproportionately to their share of the value achieved.

But the picture is not all rosy for the client. Success fees can lead to problems if not handled with care: set-up and management costs are much higher for both parties; the consultants may decide during the project that success (as defined at the outset) cannot be achieved which can lead to protracted renegotiation half-way through the project or even to the consultants withdrawing altogether; and client organizations tend to be a complex, dynamic environment in which priorities shift, once again leading to costly renegotiations.

When they work, success fees can be a hugely powerful way of building value for clients and consultants alike. The key is only to use them for the right projects—those which are of sufficient size to warrant the additional overhead involved and for which the difficulties mentioned above can be resolved to both parties' satisfaction.

Fee rates

Hourly or daily fee rates, billed at regular intervals, are still the most common way to charge for consulting (as they are for most professional services). This mechanism has some disadvantages: there is the risk that projects will overrun, causing a much higher final bill than expected, and it gives consultants little incentive to be efficient. On the other hand, it provides the necessary flexibility both for the consultants and for the clients and can be reviewed regularly against progress to ensure that costs do not run beyond what the client has budgeted. Provided the right controls are in place, this is the safe, boring way of doing it and, in my view, both parties should have a good reason before they depart from this mechanism.

Value pricing—client beware!

'Value pricing' should be the same as the success fee mechanism described above. Unfortunately the term is more often used to describe a mechanism where the consultant charges a fixed fee based on the *expected* benefit of the project. A simple example would be a cost reduction project: the consultant and the client would set a target for the cost reduction to be achieved and the consultant would charge a percentage of this saving. This is great for the consultant, who effectively gets a success fee without any of the risk and which is not directly linked to the costs incurred in delivery—the scope for high profit margins is immense (it is small wonder that most of the books about how to get rich being a consultant recommend this pricing mechanism). But it is not so good for the client unless the project proves to be more successful than they had initially envisaged. So when you hear the word 'value' mentioned in the context of billing, make sure you understand precisely what is being proposed. If in doubt, try to suggest value pricing on a relatively low value piece of work and see what reaction you get.

Conclusion on the business model

The above discussion applies to most consultants and consulting firms, but you should be aware that other models exist. These are generally encountered when dealing with highly specialized consulting firms or firms which are on the borderline between consulting and other activities. One might expect a slightly different model, for example, at a firm which deals exclusively with corporate finance advisory work, or a firm which is mainly engaged in training activities.

From time to time, a firm will appear with a 'new', 'revolutionary' way of providing consulting services, a new business model. This happened a lot, for instance, during the internet boom in the late 1990s when it was felt that there should be 'new consulting' for the 'new economy', but it is by no means limited to this period.

I would like to say that one of these firms has genuinely broken the mould, but I think that in every case that I have observed, it either has not worked or things have reverted to the norm after a few years. This is not to say that these attempts to break away from the industry do not have some benefit—the innovations are generally absorbed into the mainstream and go some way to improving how the industry operates as a whole.

For the most part, though, departures from the model I have outlined here are slight. Do not make the mistake of thinking that this means they are insignificant. These nuances can make a big difference to your relationship with a consulting firm and to performance. The sophisticated client becomes attuned to slight differences in approach and understands the impact that they are likely to have.

The consulting business model, as we have seen, colours the whole of the client-consultant relationship and yet it is the most commonly misunderstood and under-appreciated aspect of this relationship. This chapter, I hope, goes some way to addressing the issue and to equipping the client with some of the questions to ask when assessing consulting firms. The business model is, of course, only one of many factors to consider in deciding which consultants to work with. These other factors are the subject of the next chapter.

CHAPTER 2

Consulting Choices

I have often heard it said that nobody was ever fired for hiring Company X, where Company X is a major blue-chip consulting firm. I have never really understood why people say this. Firstly, I have seen little evidence to suggest it is true and quite a bit that indicates it is not, whichever consulting firm it happens to refer to. Secondly, it is at once symptomatic of the lack of knowledge many managers have about consultants and an excuse for not improving this knowledge. Consulting projects fail for many reasons, but one of the most common and most avoidable is that inappropriate consultants are chosen and critical factors which inform this choice are overlooked. It is true that the range of choices confronting a buyer of consulting can be overwhelming and, at first glance, it may be difficult to tell the difference between them. But an understanding of the characteristics which differentiate consulting firms can facilitate an informed decision. The aim of this chapter is to outline these characteristics, to suggest how they might influence your choice of consultant and then to look at the main types of consulting firm that emerge. The list of characteristics discussed here is by no means exhaustive—I have tried to select those that I believe have the greatest impact as well as those that (like the consulting business model of the previous chapter) are commonly overlooked.

Differentiating characteristics

Size

The first and most obvious factor to look at is size. This can vary from the independent consultant working part-time to the large organization employing thousands of professionals.

The main advantage of the large consulting firm is that it has the resources to tackle large and complex projects. It can also pull in additional resources should a project run into difficulties or if the scope slips. Larger firms usually (but not always) have greater prestige and this may be important in 'selling' the project within the organization or to third parties such as investors or regulators. Lastly, the larger firms usually have a broader skill base. This may not be important from the point of view of an individual project, but it can be from the perspective of the broader relationship.

The smaller firm or independent consultant often provide a much greater level of expertise and experience in the particular area they specialize in. You can also expect this expertise to be applied in the project because, rather than paying for 'a consultant', you are paying for specific individuals and their skills. The smaller firm will usually be working on relatively few projects at once and so is likely to be more focused on that particular client and have more at stake if things go wrong.

The size of a firm is not correlated to the prices it charges, contrary to what some clients seem to expect. This is hardly surprising if you think about it from a cost perspective: although smaller firms do not carry as much overhead as the big ones, this overhead is split over a much smaller cost base. Smaller firms frequently have much higher selling costs than their bigger brethren, unless they have successfully established long-term client relationships. The only substantial difference is that the smaller firm is likely to be used to working under greater resource constraints and is more likely to structure a project in a way which minimizes the resources required and consequently reduces the overall cost. Whether this is appropriate or not depends on the project and there will be projects that will simply be too big for small firms to handle on their own.

Operating model

The operating model is closely linked to the business model. The term covers the ways in which consultants interact with their clients and how they actually do their work. The main characteristics of the operating model are:

- *Team size*—this can range from body-shopping (firms which provide individual 'bodies' to fill particular roles) to the large consultant team which may be working with an equally large client team and teams of subcontractors or other specialist service providers.
- The level of *control* that the consultant has over how the work is done—projects can be run by the consultant, by the client, together, or occasionally even by a third party. In some consulting engagements the client specifies the deliverable and leaves the means up to the consultant. In others the client is more involved in the process.
- The degree of *integration* between the consultant and the client—this can range from a piece of commissioned research where the consultant will only see the client at the beginning and the end of the project, to a large client-consultant team that has daily interactions with the rest of the client organization.
- The *hierarchical spread* of the integration—how much of the organization does it cover?

- The extent to which the consultant is applying a pre-defined *process*—so-called 'cookie-cutter' consulting, though much maligned, has its place and can be a cost-effective way of delivering consulting services.
- The *project structure* favoured by the consultant

Most consulting firms will support several operating models, but will have their preferences and a habitual way of structuring projects and carrying out the work. It is important for the client to be aware of this and to assess the compatibility of the operating model or models on offer with their own culture and working practices as well as with the requirements of specific projects.

Work ethic

When I started consulting, I found myself working through the night at least once a week and was regularly putting in 18-hour days. This kind of work ethic is one of the main reasons clients opt to use consultants and in the right circumstances can ensure that a project is delivered far more rapidly than could be achieved by a purely internal approach. This is not a criticism of internal resources, it is simply that they are not usually set up to work this way and they are likely to have their normal jobs to do as well as the project.

Not all consulting firms work this way, nor is it always appropriate. For one thing, this kind of workload quickly becomes counter-productive. It is fine for a month or two, but is not really sustainable over a longer project. Secondly, it generally works best where there is a pool of relatively young consultants who are prepared to put in these kinds of hours. In my experience, not many of the senior, highly skilled consultants are prepared to work like this for long periods—and it is often precisely these people who are needed on a project. Thirdly, this approach can clash with the client's own culture: on one occasion a client told me that he was very annoyed with another consulting firm which had criticised his staff because they went home at five o'clock whereas the consultants were working until late in the evening. The consultants had not noticed that the client team were generally in the office by six in the morning whereas they came in at nine. A culture clash can be a good thing where an organization needs 'shaking up', but it can also be problematic, especially where there is a joint client-consultant team or where consultants need to work closely with people in the organization.

Consulting skills

Not all consultants began life as consultants. Indeed, most did not. The consequence of this is that many consultants come into consulting with a very limited set of consulting skills. What is the consulting skill set? This is not always easy to define, but it should certainly include client management, writing and presentation skills, project and programme structuring and management, problem structuring and solving techniques and a range of well-understood, template processes for different types of consulting project. Some firms will train their employees in this skill set, but this takes time and inevitably much of it takes place 'on the job' or can only be learnt from experience anyway.

Nor does the acquisition of these skills necessarily lead to a change of mind-set. Many consultants who have come into consulting later in their careers still see themselves as specialists first and consultants second, rather than professional consultants with specialist skills. In an ideal world, it would be best for the client to get the whole package (consulting and specialist skills), but this is not always possible. In the area of competitive intelligence, for example, the field is populated by semi-retired individuals from the industry in question who use their personal networks to gather information.

It can be difficult for the client to gauge consulting skills that a firm possesses (let alone for a specific team), especially before they have worked with them. Unfortunately, I cannot think of an easy way to make this assessment. With experience, one develops a sense for it. The development of this sense can be accelerated by paying attention to consulting skills in the selection process and in project reviews. It may also help to include a former consultant on the selection team, but even this is no guarantee because they are likely to look at things through the lens of the firm they worked for unless, of course, they have worked for several.

Professionalism

'Professionalism' means different things to different people. I am using it to refer to a combination of the skills and competencies described above, a highly developed client interface (for management and administration of projects and client relationships), a culture of excellence (or at least competence), a long-term view of the relationship and an ethic which always puts the client's broader interests first.

This may seem like quite a complex definition of professionalism, especially to those who work in the more traditional professions such as law, accounting or medicine where professionalism can be defined as adherence to a clearly defined set of standards of knowledge and behaviour. But consulting is not a profession in that it does not have these established standards and, as I have suggested before, I don't believe it can ever really be restricted in this way. So the notion of professionalism is necessarily more vague in this context, which is not to say that it is not useful.

Putting the client's interests first is possibly the most important aspect of professionalism. As a client, you should ask yourself

'Do I feel confident that the consultant would turn down work if he did not feel it was in my best interests?'. This is not a hypothetical question. Such situations arise every day and there are not all that many consultants who would say no to the prospect of several months' fees because they feel that the project would not give value for money or because they are convinced that the client's resources would be best directed elsewhere.

Even within the more professional consulting firms, not all individual consultants will be the same. If you find a truly professional consultant, it is well worth cultivating this relationship. The benefits for the client can be substantial because, broadly speaking, the less professional the consultants, the harder work they are to deal with and the less value you get from the relationship.

Most consultants you deal with are unlikely to be paragons of professionalism (not least because it comes at a price), but it helps to have an idea of where they are on the scale if you want to manage the relationship effectively.

Specialist skills and knowledge

Beyond general consulting skills, a consultant's skills and experience in specific areas is clearly a point to look at (too often it is the only thing that is looked at). Specialization comes in three flavours: industry specialization, functional specialization and task specialization. A consultant may have significant experience in reducing costs (task specialization) in the back office (functional specialization) of banks (industry specialization), but this does not necessarily qualify them to carry out an operational review of the bank's front office or to cut administrative costs in a manufacturing company. On the other hand, the experience of having worked on a particular function or task across a range of industries can be very helpful in generating new perspectives and approaches. This is one of the main benefits of using generalist consultants rather than industry insiders. Consultants will argue the benefits of the specialist or the generalist depending on which skill sets they happen to have available. As a client, you would be well-advised not to listen too hard to these arguments, but to make up your own mind as to which skill sets are needed for a project to succeed. Once this has been clearly articulated, it is much easier to probe the consultants' sales pitches and understand what skills actually are on offer.

Geographical scope

Geographical scope is the next point to check off the list. You should not assume that only the larger organizations have geographical scope. Consulting firms vary hugely in their geographical structures and even smaller firms, which may not have a presence all over the world, vary substantially in their mobility— sometimes what matters is not physical presence, but the ability to operate in the required geographies.

It is not only the breadth of a consultancy's geographical reach which may be relevant, but its density. For some projects, local knowledge and resources are key and it is useful for a consultancy to have multiple points of presence within a particular country or region.

A broad reach gives the client the opportunity to have multiple points of contact with its own organization, to use local knowledge of geographical areas in which they may not have a presence, to access the best experts regardless of location and to compare how a problem is resolved in different countries. It can also save on travel costs.

Although the advantages of a consultancy with a large geographical footprint are relatively easy to enumerate, the disadvantages tend to be more subtle. To begin with, even in the largest firms, the expertise tends to be spread quite thinly. So performance on a project can be patchy from location to location. Secondly, many firms are not as international as they might at first appear—many are made up of loosely affiliated local practices. This is particularly true of the big accounting firms, where local partners own and run the local business. Very few firms operate genuinely international practices—this is costly and can lead to issues in the command structure where local management conflicts with practice management. Lastly, many firms which claim a very broad footprint tend to be heavily concentrated in relatively few main centres. These aspects are quite difficult to discern and if geography is an issue for your organization, then it pays to work out exactly which aspects of this geography matter to you and do your homework on the consultants you intend to hire.

Relationship chemistry and culture

The existing or potential relationship chemistry between your organization and a consulting firm can be tricky to assess but is nevertheless a very important factor in choosing who you work with, especially if you are looking to develop a long-term relationship or are contemplating a critical project—no amount of technical competence can make up for a severe culture clash. So it is worth putting some time into assessing this.

Where you have an existing relationship, you at least have some data points: you can look back at the history of the relationship, you can assess the depth and breadth of it and you can come to a conclusion about its strengths and weaknesses.

It is considerably harder where a relationship does not exist. You will have to try to assess the consulting firm's culture as best you can before you enter into a relationship. Culture can partly be described in terms of the characteristics I have already outlined above, but there may be other attitudes, approaches and behaviours that do not fall under these headings. These might include personal relationships between individuals, or something as apparently mundane as an interest in sports. It is often surprising how much of an impact this sort of thing can have.

When you have some idea of the culture in the consulting firm, you can think about how this is likely to affect the relationship between that firm and your organization. Do not assume that similar cultures make for good relationships. They may well help things run more smoothly, but some friction can be helpful. I remember working on an engagement where the client team and the consulting team were competing to show that their respective approaches were better and I think the work benefited from this extra stimulus. So look for a complementary culture rather than one that is identical to your own.

I would also suggest, given the importance of this issue, that you make your assessment as real as possible. Construct some project scenarios and think about how you and the consultants are likely to respond in these situations. If you can, run these as simulations with the project teams to see how people actually respond.

Types of consultancy

Although there are consulting firms covering almost every conceivable niche, there are four main groupings that the prospective client should be aware of: full-service firms, strategy houses, IT houses and niche players. Here are some of the characteristics of each group.

Full-service firms

The full-service firms are usually tied to the large accounting firms and can provide most types of consulting service as well as accounting, audit, tax, transaction services and, in some cases, legal and regulatory services. Their business model is based on leveraging their relationships (particularly audit relationships) to sell as many other services as possible into each 'account'. They provide a convenient one-stop shop where the lazy buyer can purchase services without having to do much homework on the supplier and still be reasonably comfortable that an adequate quality of service will be provided at a relatively high price. When I say the 'lazy buyer' I do not necessarily mean this as a criticism— a degree of laziness is understandable when the client has many different priorities to juggle and an urgent requirement for a consulting project. On these occasions, the relative comfort provided by full-service firms can be a huge advantage.

The problems associated with using full-service firms have attracted much publicity in recent years. Firstly, there are the conflicts that can occur when audit and consulting are carried out by the same firm. Secondly, like many large organizations, these firms are highly political and there is considerable in-fighting over who 'owns' a particular client relationship. Huge efforts are made to avoid these types of conflict, but from what I have seen, they are never wholly successful. Thirdly, the quality of service is variable. This again is the result of the size and diversity of these firms: they cannot hope to be world class in all the areas they address. The client pays the same whether this quality is excellent or mediocre. Unless you really know the consulting firm well (or have a relationship manager who is prepared to pick and choose for you), value for money on any given project can be something of a lottery.

Strategy houses

The second group I should mention are the strategy firms. These can provoke very different reactions. For some, they represent the gold standard of consulting: the best people, the most professional standards, the most cerebral types of consulting. For others, 'strategy' carries with it connotations of nebulous concepts, 'gurus', faddish initiatives, shelves of reports and very, very expensive consultants.

The truth is somewhere in the middle, but probably does encompass elements of these two extremes. While the consultants can certainly be accused of following (and creating) the latest management fads, I have often found that clients hire them precisely because they are looking for the next big thing. Much criticism of strategy firms stems from them being used for the wrong reasons (usually political), or on projects for which they are ill-suited. The consultants are partly to blame in accepting projects, for relationship reasons, which they should never have undertaken, but this is hardly a damning indictment.

It is worth pointing out that 'strategy' consultants are not called this because they spend all their time developing 'strategies'. Most of the big strategy houses have a broad range of services. The title is due more to the fact that they deal with strategic issues, usually at board level in large organizations. To operate at this level for these kinds of clients, they need people of the highest intellectual calibre, they need professionalism and, yes, they charge astronomical fee rates—quality costs. If you have difficult problems to solve which require powerful thinking backed by rigorous analysis and in-depth research, your best bet may well be to swallow the expense and hire one of the top strategy houses. When this is not the case, you may find something less high-powered is more appropriate.

Another criticism which has been levelled at such firms is that a degree of intellectual arrogance accompanies the quality of people and the culture of excellence. On occasion this can be true. For instance, I was once told by a strategy consultant that he had just completed a project in a particular industry and was now considered one of the firm's experts in that industry. I have no doubt that he had a very good structural overview of the industry and had probably crunched vast quantities of data in his analysis of the industry dynamics. He had probably conducted interviews with people in his client's organization and elsewhere. But, no matter how intellectually acute the individual in question, the knowledge to be gained from this type of structural approach is, in my view, necessarily less complete (and certainly less nuanced) than that of someone who has been exposed to the industry for many years, even if that person is of a lower intellectual calibre. The best consultants know this and strive to achieve a synthesis between their own strengths and the experience and knowledge already present in their client's organization.

IT consultants

When I started consulting, firms that specialized in IT were very much niche players. Since then, the big IT firms have come to dominate the consulting landscape and account for an ever-increasing share of the global consulting market.

This is hardly surprising: the improvements in efficiency and effectiveness that technology can offer most businesses are enormous and those ignoring it would quickly be rendered obsolete. At the same time, the complexity of this technology is so great and is evolving so quickly, and the risks involved in deploying it are so high that it makes no sense for organizations to maintain all the necessary expertise internally. This is where the IT firms come in.

These firms generally have quite flat structures with large armies of people at the base of the pyramid and very strong operating procedures in place to manage them. This is what is needed to deliver large scale systems implementations, which is what these firms primarily do. This business model is also extremely profitable, as I mentioned earlier, as long as these armies are kept busy.

Some of these firms have evolved to the point where consulting has become a peripheral activity (outsourcing, turnkey projects etc.). Some of these new business models have proved powerful, but I shall not dwell on them here because because I think they fall outside the scope of this book.

What the prospective client should remember is that these firms' reason for existence is to implement and integrate large-scale IT solutions. Anything else they do is peripheral to this activity or is done with the express aim of winning more implementation work. This is not to say that they are necessarily bad at other areas of consulting—they often have excellent process and productivity consultants, for instance—but it does mean that these are not their main areas of focus except where they help them sell or execute systems projects.

Most managers I talk to also have stories of these large-scale, consultant-run systems projects going horribly wrong and costing vast amounts of money. Sometimes this is the fault of the consultants. Usually the blame can be shared. Often they are ill-conceived (albeit with the best intentions), inherently risky, with many unknowns, and have only a marginal chance of succeeding as intended. On the other hand, when they work, they can be transformative.

Niche players

The third group, which probably includes the majority of consultants, are the niche players. These are often (but by no means always) small firms or individual consultants who have concentrated on developing a very high degree of expertise in an industry, functional or process niche. With these consultants it is important to remember that the narrower the specialism, the less likely they are to have developed consulting skills and operating procedures. This is simply because a high level of expertise takes time and focus to acquire and develop. This is not to say that specialist firms do not provide value. It merely means that the relationship needs to be structured in such a way as to play to their strengths (content rather than form) and that the client needs to allow more time to manage them, especially when dealing with a large number of such suppliers.

The aim of this chapter was to provide prospective clients with a set of criteria by which to distinguish and select consultants. In the next chapter I will describe the 'consulting process'—the steps which occur from identification of a set of requirements through to the completion and review of a consulting assignment. I would advise you to select (or at least short list) which consulting firms you want to work with, and in which circumstances before this process begins i.e. before you have identified any specific requirements. There are three reasons for this. Firstly, once there is a perceived need, there is usually no time to perform a review of what is on offer. The choice then becomes limited to whatever happens to be available at the time, which is the wrong way round. Secondly, many of the characteristics described above are not project specific, but relate to the fit between the client organization and consulting firm. These are the characteristics which tend to fade into the background when faced with a specific and urgent need. Thirdly, a preselection permits early communication when requirements do come up, which in turn improves the requirements definition and allows the consultants to earmark resources for the project. In other words, an early shortlist can greatly increase the probability of getting the right team in place when an urgent need arises.

CHAPTER 3

The Consulting Process

Every consulting project is different: firms take different approaches to problems, clients have different requirements and the types of work differ, as do investments in time and money. That said, at the core of every project it is possible to discern a series of activities which, from the client's perspective, make up a generic consulting process. The variation in these activities is mainly a matter of who (client or consultant) is carrying them out and the degree of emphasis and effort placed on each step. When projects go wrong, it is often because one of these activities has been neglected or not carried out correctly. A familiarity with the process should make you more aware of the warning signs which, if acted upon quickly, can help prevent problems arising. The aim of this chapter is to go through the components of the process and to point out where things typically go wrong at each step.

Most consulting firms have some kind of process diagram which comes out during training sessions and the same is true for those clients who train managers to work with consultants. Most of the diagrams I have seen are too simplistic and too consultant-focused to be of much use. The process I set out here is more client-centric and a little more complex (in that it contains more steps)—this allows you to select the steps that are relevant rather than create new ones to fill the gaps.

Client Activities in a Consulting Project

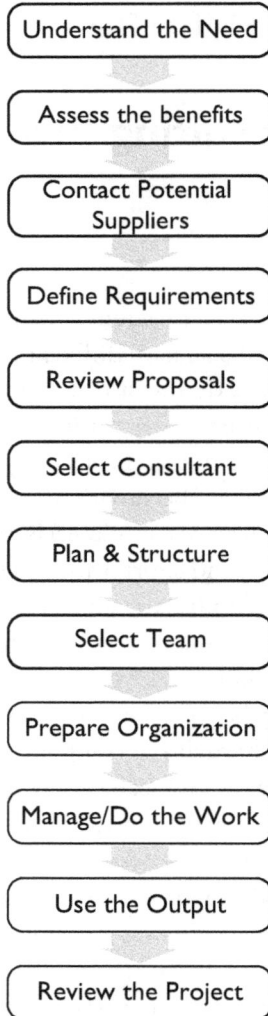

Understand the Need

Assess the benefits

Contact Potential Suppliers

Define Requirements

Review Proposals

Select Consultant

Plan & Structure

Select Team

Prepare Organization

Manage/Do the Work

Use the Output

Review the Project

Understanding the need

I shall assume here that most readers know how to conduct a needs assessment and shall confine myself to a few points that I think are particularly relevant to this stage in a consulting project.

Firstly, consultants are brought in to deal with avoidable emergencies far too often. Although rapid response and deployment are among the benefits of using consultants, using them exclusively in this way is not in the client's best interest: it is much more expensive, it greatly increases the risk of failure or of poor quality and it leads to initiatives being prioritized by urgency rather than by importance to the client organization. It is also often the result of clients initiating projects in-house without the necessary skills or planning and then bringing consultants in to fix them when they go wrong. It is far better to be more thorough in the assessment of the need at the outset and to be realistic about the skills and resources needed to carry it out. Of course, you are unlikely to succeed in this every time, but it would be good if this could be the norm rather than the exception.

So, in assessing the need for consultants, if at all possible try to take a longer term perspective—it pays to think ahead. It also pays to take a broad perspective: most large organizations have quite a few initiatives and projects running at any one time and more in the pipeline. These can be managed as a portfolio and the need for consulting resources should be assessed in this context.

A good relationship with a consulting firm can also prove very useful at this stage: they can advise about project prioritization and provide an external view of the organization's capability to deliver, as well as identifying areas where external help will be needed and how best to obtain this help. Most consultants will not charge for this sort of advice (unless it turns into a full-time job) because they view it as part of their relationship management.

It helps to have a consultant you can trust (and here I mean an individual rather than a firm) for this kind of discussion and not one who is simply trying to pump as many services as possible into your organization. But if you only know consultants in the latter category, you should still ask—you are under no obligation to follow their advice.

Assessing the benefits

When considering any kind of project, whether there are consultants involved or not, it is normal to assess how you stand to benefit. A good understanding of the potential benefits not only helps with the prioritization of your project portfolio, but also influences the structuring and resourcing of the project so that these are proportional to the gains. Some organizations are very sophisticated in this area, with tools and processes in place to carry out fairly complex assessments. For those who are not as sophisticated, consultants can provide support with the technical analysis and quantification.

These techniques have their uses: they inform your thinking, they encourage a more rigorous consideration of the issues, they can be helpful in presenting your project and they can be used as a basis for tracking. But, for most consulting projects, my advice would be not to overdo it on the technical analysis: scorecards, NPVs and sensitivity analysis do support the decision-making process but can create an illusion of precision and objectivity that can blind you to a far more messy reality.

The most common problem at this stage is that benefits are overestimated (and costs are underestimated). It is difficult to tell managers who are trying to justify a project which they feel is important to treat projected benefits with caution, nor is there an easy set of checks and balances that can be used to counter this tendency. The best advice that I have been given is to make sure as many eyes as possible take a look at the proposal and check the track record of the proposer—some people seem to be serial optimists. If you have to run projects frequently, it is worth reviewing the variance between estimates and actual outcomes. Quite often there is a fairly clear bias and you can correct for it in future estimates. For instance, if you find the benefits are usually 5%-10% lower than estimates, then run your normal benefits assessment and reduce it by 10%.

It is also a good idea to remain aware of the potential variance in outcomes. People often spend a lot of time trying to pin down the most likely benefit or cost numbers but forget that the reality might turn out to be plus or minus 200% of these 'best estimates'.

Contacting potential suppliers

This step in the process can be broken down further into four sub-steps: identification, short listing (i.e. deciding who you are going to talk to), contact and dialogue.

Identifying potential suppliers is easy when you are looking for consultants to perform a recognized service for which there is an established, competitive market, or where you already maintain relationships with consultants.

When you want to do something that has not been done before, or you need a very specific set of skills or experience, or if it is an area where supply is constrained, you may find that it is difficult to find precisely what you are looking for. At times, a suitable supplier may not exist at all and you will have to find creative ways to address your issue. This may mean resourcing the work internally. If this is not possible, you may find that the best solution is to break the problem up and use different consultancies for each piece. Or it may be best to select a consultancy that has some of what you require and that you feel comfortable with, and work with them to develop a solution that will cover everything.

Whether it is easy or difficult to find the consultants you want, it is a good idea to do this as early as possible. That way you will be aware of any potential problems early on, they can help you shape your thinking about the project and you can get an idea of where their strengths and weaknesses lie before you invite them to make a proposal. For many types of consulting project, the consultants will have considerably more experience of addressing the issue than you do (that's why you're hiring them), and their input at the structuring stage of the project can be invaluable.

When there are few suppliers available, there is relatively little selection to do (in some cases you may even need to sell your project to them), but usually some selection is involved. This usually occurs in cycles: initial selection of consultants to talk to, short listing of those who you want to have deeper discussions with, selection of the ones who you will invite to propose and finally your choice of the one you will work with. In multi-phase projects, this can be repeated at the start of each phase. All this can be a huge drain on your time. So, once you know roughly how wide your choice is, it is worth thinking about how you are going to manage the selection process. You will need to strike a balance between keeping your options open and the depth of information gained. Remember that the more consultants you are dealing with, the less time you will have to speak to each one and get the information you need to make your final decision. It is also worth keeping in mind that the main goal of the initial discussions will be to select the consultants you will work with and so you should ask questions that will actually make a difference to this selection—I have seen lengthy selection processes at the end of which it was almost impossible to make a decision because the questions asked, though interesting and informative, did not help distinguish between suppliers.

At some point during all this, you will have to initiate contact with prospective suppliers. Most consultants are only too eager to hear from potential clients, so this is generally quite straightforward. But here too a little forethought can save a lot of time and money: despite the efforts of some consulting firms, consultants are not clones and who you talk to initially can make an enormous difference to how smoothly things go thereafter. Your worst case scenario is to call the switchboard of the consulting firm and ask them to direct you to someone who knows about the subject matter you are interested in. You may be lucky, but nine times out of ten you will end up speaking to the person who happens to be in the office when you call. And you may end up getting stuck with that person because consultancy incentive schemes can at times encourage territorial behaviour.

If it is at all possible, try to identify the individual you want to speak to before you call. This need not be the person who would actually do the work, but it should be someone who can advise you on who the right person might be and who is able to channel your inquiry. The best way to do this is via a personal recommendation and introduction. Where this is not possible, you may be able to get a name by talking to other companies that have worked with the consulting firm on similar projects, from articles and newsletters, or from the consultant's marketing materials.

The nature of the dialogue you have with consultants at this stage will vary depending on the type of project that you have in mind. Typically, the client will be trying to find out all they can about the consulting firm's capabilities, their approach to the problem and how well they fit. The consultants, on the other hand, will want to understand the background to the work, the client's current thinking about the problem, the purchasing decision process (and the players involved) and any further opportunities that might exist within the client organization. They may also be identifying what resources they can bring to bear on the project. The only suggestion I have here (beyond what I have already said about selection) is that it helps to keep an open mind—sometimes a consulting firm which doesn't score well on your initial criteria may approach the problem in a different way that plays to their strengths and is also to your advantage.

Defining the requirements

The issue here is getting the right level of detail. Requirement definition tends either not to happen at all or to involve such levels of detail as to be incomprehensible and largely unmanageable. The latter is particularly true of some public sector selection procedures. A definition of requirements for consulting services should contain the following:

- Background and context of the project in brief
- General and specific objectives
- Concrete deliverables
- Timescales
- Approximate budget and an indication of the internal resources which will be made available
- Any particular requirements/ constraints regarding working practices, billing etc.
- Details of technical requirements where applicable
- Explicit identification of areas of uncertainty or ambiguity

It is not generally advisable for the requirements document to specify how the consultants are to carry out the work or attempt to micromanage the project before its inception.

This is the latest stage in the process at which discussions with the consultants should begin (earlier would be better) and requirements should be subjected to substantial review and revision based on discussions with the consultants. Such involvement greatly reduces the risks of misunderstanding and misalignment which are common when consultants are presented with a project definition as a *fait accompli*.

The proposal

Proposals used to be sales documents which attempted to persuade the client to buy a firm's services. This is rarely the case nowadays, even in tender situations, because most of the selling has been done much earlier through presentations and discussions. The proposal merely formalizes these and, once agreed, is the contract between the consultant and the client.

From the consultant's point of view, the proposal is the key document which guides them throughout the project. It is a direct response to the requirements (which may take the form of a Request for Proposal or an Invitation to Tender), sets the terms of reference for the consulting team and forms the basis for the detailed project plan which follows. A proposal should include:

- A review of the background and requirements with comments and observations
- Objectives and deliverables as understood by the consultant
- An outline of the approach to be taken covering the skills required, the main areas of work, the overall structure of

the project and a description of how collaboration and interaction between the consultants and the client organization will take place

- An outline work plan which should be sufficiently detailed to provide a confident estimate of the resources required and the timing of these requirements and set out key milestones and dates for deliverables
- The management structure for the project covering responsibilities and accountabilities, a description of the key roles, content, attendance and frequency of key meetings and mechanisms for formal and informal communications
- A description of the key people who will be involved from the consulting side. (Some consultancies are reluctant to provide this because it limits their resourcing flexibility. As a client, you should either insist on it or require the right to have the final say in team selection)
- An explanation of how the project is to be tracked and assessed, including requirements for final and interim sign-offs
- A description of key areas of risk and how they will be managed
- Change management procedures

Given the importance of the proposal to the success of the project, it is essential that the client be 100% happy with it before the project gets underway. This is easier said than done: it is often tempting in the rush to get the project started, to leave 'minor' areas of doubt for later discussions, especially when multiple proposals are being reviewed. Inevitably, it is these 'minor' points which come back to haunt you later. Of course, it would be naïve to suggest that once the proposal has been accepted, it is set in stone and nothing will be changed. Consulting projects are far too complex and generally involve too many unknowns for that to be realistic. But it does make life much easier for all involved if such changes are made from a solid base and with the full understanding of the implications.

Consultant selection

I have little to say about the selection process itself: this can vary in complexity from a single manager making a decision to a scenario that involves multiple panels and committees, and sometimes specialist consultants who advise on the selection. The key, as always, it to opt for a process that is appropriate to the project in question. The criteria used to select a consulting firm for a particular project are specific to that project and are usually related to the consultants' technical ability to carry out the work within the budget the client has set for it. There is, however, another set of criteria, which might be termed the 'soft' or 'relationship' criteria, that are often not explicitly considered in the selection process. The terms used to describe these criteria include 'style', 'culture', 'fit', 'familiarity', 'compatibility' or 'chemistry'. There is some justification for this exclusion: one of the benefits of using consultants is that they should come with relatively few strings attached and the client does not expect to have to manage them as he does his own employees—consultants are supposed to save managers time. So managers frequently leave the 'soft' side of the consulting project to the consultants themselves and focus on managing the objectives and the deliverables and on ensuring value for money.

There are two problems with this. Firstly, the success of most consulting projects depends heavily on the quality and nature of the interaction between the consultant and the organization.

Consequently the chemistry between the consultants and the organization's employees is critical in ensuring this success. This does not mean that the relationship should necessarily be a cosy one—as I mentioned in the previous chapter, in some circumstances an atmosphere of competition or confrontation can be beneficial—but it does mean that the client should be aware of how the consultant is viewed within the organization, the personalities of the consultants who will work on the project, the style that the consultants propose to adopt in their interaction with employees and what is likely to happen when this style encounters the organization's culture.

The second problem with the 'hard' approach is that objectives, deliverables and value for money tend to be very project-focused criteria and do not take into account the broader relationship an organization may have or may wish to have with the consultancy. This can have very practical implications: in many projects, the consultants' existing knowledge of the client organization (gained from previous engagements) can largely offset and even outweigh any technical advantage that another consultancy might bring to bear. This is particularly true of projects involving organizational change and IT systems. Where a consultancy has carried out similar projects in other parts of the organization, they are better positioned on the learning curve than one which has not and may even be able to merge the two projects, gaining some economies of scale. At the very least it should be possible for projects carried out by the same firm to share some of the administrative overheads and exchange some key learning points.

These softer considerations should be among the most important factors to look at in selecting consultants for a project because, for most consulting assignments, it should be possible to find several prospective suppliers of similar technical competence and price. So the relationship criteria are, in these cases, the ones which swing the decision.

As I mentioned at the end of the last chapter, the weighting between hard and soft criteria influences the timing of the selection: where the relationship criteria are more important, the consultant can be selected much earlier in the process, before the project has been fully defined and structured. This greatly facilitates the early involvement of the consultant, which generally means that the project will be planned and structured better (not because consultants are necessarily better at this, but simply because more information is available and there is more opportunity to discuss the issues), the organization has more time to prepare and the consultant has more time to line up the right people to carry out the work. It is also a token of confidence in the consulting firm which most consultants should appreciate.

Planning and structuring the project

The detailed planning step goes some way beyond the broader scoping which should have occurred before. It involves four main activities:

- Breaking down the work in detail (this is the only way I have found to really get a handle on how much work is to be done and the consequent resource requirements)
- Structuring the work: grouping the tasks so that they can be assigned to individuals and teams and ordering these tasks in a sequence which will optimize the use of resources while taking into account timescales, costs and dependencies.

- Designing and implementing procedures for progress reporting and tracking, change management and issues management and escalation.
- Designing and implementing management and reporting structures.

Project planning and management is a discipline in its own right and there is a considerable literature on it for those who want to go into more detail. I cannot go into it here, but I would like to point out a few things to watch out for that are particularly relevant to consulting projects.

Get the level of detail right

Consulting projects tend to involve quite a high level of uncertainty about the work involved. The amount of work to be done on one area will often depend on the output from another. Indeed, the whole scope of the project can change as a consequence of one key discovery or piece of analysis. This often leads to one of two responses: not doing the planning at all or over-planning. Both can be disastrous. It is essential to go down to a fine level of detail when breaking down the work, but it is equally essential to come up several levels when looking at phasing and key decision points—otherwise the project gets bogged down in its own management.

Don't underestimate the effort needed to get the team working properly

Consulting projects commonly involve significant interaction between the consultants and the organization. In larger projects, this can extend to a joint client-consultant team and very large projects may involve people at all levels from different parts of the organization and several consulting firms. The potential for friction in what is often a high pressure environment is enormous. On the other hand, the synergies between the consultants' skills and experience and the client team members' knowledge of the organization and its activities are often the key to achieving the benefits.

The friction can be reduced by careful team selection (more on this later), clarity of roles and responsibilities, adequate preparation of the client team members and team-building at the start of the project. I have occasionally worked for clients who deliberately created this friction in the hope that it would challenge people and trigger creativity. On the face of it, this seems to make some sense, but it is risky and I have yet to see it produce a satisfactory result.

For the client team members, participation in a consulting project can be quite traumatic: they are plucked out of the comfort zone of their regular job and team; in some cases, they have no certainty of returning to their previous role when the project is completed; many are not accustomed to the structures and disciplines of project-based work and they are expected to perform unfamiliar tasks with unfamiliar people who do not even share the same organizational culture. When someone has all these things playing on their mind, they can hardly be expected to perform at their best.

So make sure client team members get the support they need to overcome these obstacles: they should have a clear idea of where they will go after the project is complete (or at least of the opportunities available to them). They should discuss with their managers how the project can benefit their career progression and how these personal development opportunities fit with the individual's hopes and expectations. Where they lack particular skills, these shortcomings should be addressed before the project begins in earnest. The first two actions can only be carried out by the individual's own managers, the third can be taken in hand by the consultants as part of the team- building process, but only if it is planned into the project.

Any project which is not a one-man show will go through a team-building process. This will happen regardless of whether or not it is formalized and deliberately structured. Some kind of formal process is usually better: when there is no formalized team-building, it is slow and unstructured and occurs while the project work is being carried out, thus causing a major distraction from the work in hand. I have seen projects where the individuals involved only really began working as a team towards the end of the project. A formal team-building process can be carried out quickly, planned into the project and controlled. So don't skimp on the team-building at the beginning of the project, because you will pay for it later.

Use clear project management structures to combat complexity

The complexities that can arise in managing a consulting project should not be underestimated. It is not unusual for projects to get bogged down because too many people in the client organization get involved in trying to direct activities. When the project is simple (for instance a market analysis in which most of the consultants' work is external to the organization) and the deliverable is a report, such complexities are less of an issue. But when consultants are more intimately involved with the organization and the deliverable is a change in the organization itself, then the project is exposed to multiple influences, vested interests, personal agendas and company politics.

In such circumstances, the structuring of the project and particularly of the management of the project is of critical importance. You need to design a structure that allows for substantial involvement by all those who can make a contribution, but maintains clarity of control and direction. There is no prescription for this because it depends too much on the particular circumstances of the project, but I can provide a rough checklist of things to consider:

- *A single project director*—responsible for delivery.
- *A steering group (and subgroups, if the project is divided into workstreams)*—this group is responsible for strategy rather than delivery and provides an opportunity to get key people on-side by giving them a say in the direction the project takes.
- *Advisory groups*—for people who should not influence the project directly, but whose views may be of value.
- *Workshops*—also a good way to include people without making them part of the project team.
- *Spin-off projects*—sub-projects or workstreams occasionally acquire a life of their own and become too big to be subordinated to the initial project. When this happens, you should accept this reality and create a separate, parallel project.
- *Clear guidelines on confidentiality*—who should know what and who decides?
- *Joint consultant/client team leaders*—this requires more time and there is always the risk of friction, but I have seen it work well in the past where the two team leaders have formed an effective sub-team to lead the project.
- *Allocation of deliverables outside the main project team (i.e. getting other people to do some of the work)*—this can simplify the project management and structure, but bears with it the risks inherent in any external dependencies.

- *Specific 'clients' for specific project deliverables*—provided the clients can be kept under control, this can be a good way of encouraging greater buy-in within the organization.

Ensure that there are adequate project management skills in place

As I said at the start of this section, there are many aspects of project management and structuring which could be discussed here, but which fall under the more general project management discipline. If a project is to succeed, these project management skills must be present. In most cases, the consultant will be well versed in project management, but not always. For instance, a specialized consultant who is being brought in because of his area of expertise may not have the occasion or need to develop these skills. Equally, a single consultant or small group of consultants who have been brought in to play a role in a larger client project may not be in a position to influence the management of the project. Even where the consultant has the skills and is in a position to perform this role, it does not absolve the client of all responsibility in this area: just as the client would have difficulty in planning the work of the consultants, the consultants are unlikely to know enough of the client organization to prepare the plan by themselves. In most cases this should be a joint effort.

Include project management resources in the plan

I have often seen project plans which make no allowance for the effort required to plan and manage the project. They assume that, once the plan is in place, the project can go ahead. But project planning and management continues throughout the project and does require considerable effort, particularly from the more senior people involved. I would strongly recommend that you reduce the management workload for these senior people by planning in some more junior resources to handle the administrative work. If you do not, this workload ends up being taken up by the senior people who, frankly, have better things to do.

Team selection

The importance of getting the right team to carry out the project can hardly be overstated. Unfortunately, team selection is complicated by all kinds of constraints. Perhaps the greatest constraint is time—if there is enough time, other constraints such as people's availability can be overcome.

So if the project is important but not urgent, you should be prepared to wait until you get the right team in place and avoid artificial deadlines. Even in the most urgent projects, the time factor is not entirely out of the client's control: identification of potential team members can begin very early in the process, even when the terms of reference are still vague; having information about the consultants employed by the firm or firms being considered can also buy some time; and you do not have to accept the team composition that the consultant proposes at the outset— you should review it and, where necessary, challenge it.

Equally, if the project involves team members from the client, these should not just be a random group of whoever is available at the time.

Team selection and project planning tend to go hand-in-hand. Although it is preferable to pick a team for the project rather than the other way round, the definition of roles within the project structure should take into account the strengths and weaknesses of the individuals involved (and hopefully play to their strengths). Nor should task-related skills be the only consideration in selecting the team—a good team is a balance of experience, energy and different personalities.

The time and care spent choosing the team will, of course, depend on the size of the project and its importance to the organization. But even for smaller projects, a little thought can yield considerable benefits and need not involve a huge effort.

Preparing the organization

The amount that needs to be done here depends again on the type and size of project you envisage. If the project is relatively large and high-profile, this step is essential. When it is not done or when it is inadequately implemented, it can result in hostility within the organization, lack of co-operation, confusion, inefficiency and culture shock—and, of course, it makes any implementation of the project's recommendations extremely difficult.

The objective is to create an internal environment that will allow the project to be executed as efficiently and as smoothly as possible. In practical terms, this means informing people about why the project is being carried out, how it will work, what levels of disruption (if any) can be expected, what will be expected of them in terms of participation in the project or contributions to it and who they should talk to if they have issues, questions or concerns. Most importantly, if at all possible, make sure people understand how the project could benefit them and what they need to do to ensure this happens. Not everyone will need to know everything, but the consultants and clients should at least discuss who will be told what and when.

The final responsibility for this preparation falls squarely on the client—the consultants can advise, but they cannot carry out the task themselves because it must come from within the organization to be effective.

Doing the work

You might think that if all the pre-project work is done well, the project is almost guaranteed to run smoothly. Unfortunately this is not the case. Every project carries with it a certain amount of execution risk which is unavoidable. The good news is that all the preparatory steps can go a long way to limiting this risk and provide the best possible basis for the project to succeed.

The involvement of the client in carrying out the work can vary hugely: at one extreme, the consultant will be given a task and will go away and do it, reporting back when it is done; at the other, client-consultant teams under the direct supervision of the project director will be working closely with your organization. The first case is likely to involve a more discrete piece of work and the risk should be fairly contained. But this does not mean it is not there and sometimes the consequences when things go wrong can be worse, simply because you don't see it coming. So, even with projects where the consultant can legitimately expect to be left to get on with it, the wise client will insist on regular progress updates.

For projects that involve more of the client organization, all the normal project and programme management principles apply and I do not propose to go into them here. But there are a few points that are worth mentioning, either because they are often neglected or because I have found them particularly helpful in reducing the risks and making projects run smoothly:

- *Allow adequate time for project set-up*—this includes the team-building mentioned earlier, the implementation and fine-tuning of the reporting and management structures, familiarization with the project plan and allocation of tasks. When a project is on a tight budget, this tends to be the first thing to be cut—it is almost always a false economy.

- *Make sure the objectives and resources are aligned*—it is only natural when commissioning a project to try to get the best value for your money. Unfortunately, it is easy to go too far and doom a project to failure before it has even started by not giving it enough time or resources to achieve its objectives or by making these unachievable. It can be a fine balance. A key consideration should be the downside risk if the project fails. Where this is very large, it may actually be better to over-resource the project. Where you are determined to set stretch targets, you should consider setting aside a sizeable (and secret) contingency in case things do go off the rails.
- *Ensure that the project is tracked*—planning to track the project is not the same as tracking it. I have seen projects where tracking has been planned in at the start, but has then been neglected once work is underway, or where the participants just go through the motions. A clear idea of what is going on and what progress is being made is essential if you are to respond quickly to any issues. This means that someone has to collect and collate the information and that the project managers have to make time to review it and make decisions based upon it.
- *Tackle issues early*—sometimes they go away of their own accord, but I wouldn't count on it.
- *Keep it flexible*—the more flexibility you build into the plan, the better able you will be to react when events take an unforeseen course. With larger projects, you rarely end up going exactly where you planned to go, but the

end result need not be any worse (and may be better) if you are willing to adapt.

- *Ensure that value is delivered throughout the project*—projects can run into difficulties for all kinds of reasons which may have nothing to do with the project itself. For instance, I have been involved in three projects in which the client company became an acquisition target and the projects had to be curtailed or postponed. If a project can yield useful outputs throughout its course (and with a little creative thinking this is usually possible), the investment has not been for nothing, even if it has to be cut short.

- *Avoid project blinkers*—when a consulting project is running, it is natural to be focused on the objectives and the tasks in hand. This focus can lead to a sort of tunnel vision in which anything not directly relevant to getting the work done is ignored. But there are many factors beyond the 'work' that can make a difference to the project's success or failure: the political and emotional context in which the project is operating is often key and may override the rational, almost mechanistic way in which many projects are managed. Communications are also very important—when you fail to communicate, people fill in the blanks with rumour and conjecture that can undermine the project. And occasionally reviewing whether the project is really creating as much value as it could (as opposed to whether it is meeting its deadlines) can be beneficial. In short, keep your eyes and ears open.

Implementation and change management

So the project has run its course and the consultants have delivered their final report and recommendations. What happens next? Perhaps the most common criticism of consultants is that they do not implement their recommendations. Stories of consulting reports which are gathering dust on the shelf (or being used as doorstops) rarely fail to raise a wry smile of familiarity. The consultants, on the other hand, could argue with some justification that the clients in question have only themselves to blame: it is they who define the outputs at the start of a project and it is they who decide how this output is to be used.

But blaming each other does little to solve what is a fairly complex problem—neither the client nor the consultant want a report that gathers dust. If you wish to avoid this situation, it is best to start by looking at why it occurs.

Firstly, report production is the cheapest form of consulting. When faced with a client who has a tight budget or who is negotiating hard on price, the consultant will scale back his proposal in the hope that once the initial report is complete there will be sufficient momentum to sell an implementation phase. It takes a brave consultant to tell the client that he is wrong and that the benefits from a report will be small—there is always the fear that if he asks for more, he will get nothing. Consultants often fall into the trap of selling a report or assessment phase at a loss in the expectation that future work will result. Unfortunately, the second phase does not often materialize because, I think, the preparation of a report does not in itself create much momentum for action. The client may intend to act upon the findings himself, but often becomes distracted by other, more pressing matters until the report is no longer current enough to be of much use.

It could also be argued that, rather than writing a report (which can be a lengthy process), the consultants' time would be put to better use preparing the implementation of the findings. In many cases this is probably true, but there is one obstacle which tends to block what would otherwise be a sensible course of action—the client wants the report. A report is often the only tangible output of a consulting assignment, the only thing that the client can hold up, point to and say 'this is what I got for my money'. The client may need this to justify his own decision to carry out the project. So, even if it is a suboptimal use of resources, the report ends up getting written and the more substantial it is, the more comfortable the client feels. I have heard people refer to this (ironically, I hope) as 'dollars per page' consulting.

The focus on reports is also due to an excessive emphasis on the rational and analytical in the work of consultants. This is probably more the consultants' fault than the clients': consultancies tend to hire very intelligent and often highly academically qualified individuals. Such individuals tend to gravitate naturally to what they know best—analysis and problem-solving. Although there will be instances when these types of skills are precisely what the client needs, more often they are only part of the solution. There is little point sending a rocket scientist to re-organize a sales force or to instil momentum into a stalled initiative. Such assignments require relatively little analysis, but do require strong organizational skills and the ability to make things happen. They need a doer rather than a thinker. If you are a client who is considering such a project, the best advice is to be clear in your own mind about the type of people who will be needed to carry it out and to be sure that the consulting firm you choose has this kind of person available.

The emphasis on rational analysis can also be seen on the client side. It is a common error to believe that once a problem has been thoroughly analysed and solutions proposed, one is well on the way to achieving this solution. But to decide that something should be done is not the same as doing it, even if resources are available for implementation. Organizations are complex entities with very strong political and emotional undercurrents that must be addressed if anything is to be achieved. And the resources earmarked for implementation usually represent only a small part of the effort needed to take an initiative to completion. Readers who have tried to run an organizational change project will be familiar with what I am talking about here.

For those who have not had this or a similar experience, the following illustration might help. Imagine a simple project—making a cup of coffee. Unless you are a coffee aficionado who is very particular about how their coffee is ground and brewed, this should be a fairly easy task: you go to the vending machine, select the coffee, press the switch and the coffee appears.

Now place the same, simple task in an organizational context with two constraints (which are typical of the challenges encountered in implementing consulting recommendations)—everybody has to take the coffee the same way and they must be persuaded (not ordered) to do this.

The coffee is to be shared by 20 people. You have hired an expert coffee consultant who has provided a report and recommendations on the best coffee to use for the group in question and how best to make and serve it. Now it is time for implementation: first, you have to convince everyone that the consultant's recommendations are right. If you succeed in this, some people will still question why they should be having coffee, rather than tea or fruit juice. Others will not want to drink anything at all. Some will want milk, others will want sugar or sweeteners. Some will like it strong and others weak. Persuading all of these people to drink the coffee and to take it the same way is no easy task, especially since the arguments are not likely to be even remotely rational. Once everyone has been convinced, you can begin the discussion about how much coffee each person gets. Finally, to complete the analogy, imagine that all the people you are talking to about coffee are simultaneously engaged in other conversations and activities while you are talking to them.

This is what you have to deal with when implementing any project in an organization, although the project and the constraints are usually somewhat greater in magnitude (try replacing the word 'coffee' above with 'IT system' or 'marketing strategy'). A good implementation consultant will have the experience to help their client through this minefield, but they do not have a magic wand and the desired result will only be achieved if the client has the drive, commitment, patience and pragmatism to see it through to the end.

Some people will argue that in an organizational context it is possible to simply order people to do things and that this would clear up the whole mess described above. This is only true to some extent and in some organizations—one would imagine, for instance, that this command and control approach would work much better in the army than in an advertising agency. In most organizations, though, when people feel undervalued (as they do when decisions are taken out of their hands) they start to underperform. This kind of reaction is exacerbated when they feel that the views of strangers (consultants) are being put before those of the employees. Bear in mind too that when you are using the output of a consulting project, in many cases you will have to persuade people who do not have to take orders from you (like your boss or their boss). Persuasion may well be your only option.

I began the discussion above by talking about discrete projects where consultants deliver a report or a set of recommendations and leave the client to act upon them. In many cases, of course, the consultants are also involved in implementing their proposals. The most difficult implementations (and also the most common) are those that involve making changes to the client organization. These may involve systems, processes, products, markets, functions, organizational structure and strategy.

In an ideal world, once something is implemented it should stay implemented. But with organizational change (which is where much consulting is applied), even when it is successfully implemented, it is surprising how often things slip back to something that very closely resembles the way they were before, once the consultants leave. There are many reasons why this happens, but these do not include the size of the project, the investment made or the project sponsor's place in the organizational pecking order. Nor is a 'burnt bridges' approach a guarantee that the change will stick, or at least it hasn't been on most occasions that I have seen it tried.

Despite constant and sometimes vocal criticism of the *status quo*, very few people embrace change, especially when that change is brought about by someone who is external to the organization. This reaction is often not even conscious—I have seen people who have been avid supporters of a consulting project slip back into old habits as soon as any difficulties are encountered with the new way of doing things. Where the project has been about productivity improvement, you often encounter a 'supervision benefit' followed by a 'supervision deficit': while the consultants are there, they are constantly monitoring performance and productivity to assess whether the measures taken are working; it is hardly surprising in this situation that people up their performance and then slack off when the monitors disappear. But I have found that the most common reason is simply that the time and effort needed to bed a change in is underestimated.

Of course, like many of the issues discussed in this chapter, this one also applies to projects where consultants are not involved, but the external element does tend to exacerbate the problem. Below are a few suggestions to help you deal with it. The list is by no means exhaustive (change management is a big area), but, especially if you combine them with the suggestions on 'doing the work' above, they should provide a good starting point.

- *Sell the benefits to those involved*—I know I have said this before, but the point bears repeating. It is not enough to convince people of the benefits the project brings to the organization, they have to see how it will improve things for them and that this improvement is significant enough to make an effort for. It is also important to ensure you deliver on these benefits and then get people to confirm that these benefits are real.
- *Keep an eye on the context of the project*—for the consultants it is usually easy to focus on the work in hand, but the employees in the client organization are often subject to all kinds of additional concerns and influences. It is important not to ignore these. Equally, it is important to remember that the project (especially a long one) exists in a context of constantly shifting priorities.
- *Be realistic about the investment profile*—anyone who has been involved in a construction project knows that much of the time, effort and money go into the finishing. The same is true of consulting projects and you should plan your investment accordingly.
- *Taper the consultant involvement*—the abrupt departure of the consultant team can often trigger a reversion to the *status quo*. It is better for the consultants to gradually

reduce their involvement so that people don't notice when they are no longer there.

- *Reinforce the change and plan for 'aftercare'*—set up a regular review to ensure things are bedding in and head off any issues as they arise (this is different from the project review discussed in the next section). This can be tapered too (once a week for a month and then once a month for three months, or something similar). And ensure that the consultants are available to provide support if anything arises out of these reviews for which they are needed.

With all the discussion of issues, problems and difficulties in this section, I appreciate that it can come across as very negative. It may leave you feeling that it is a miracle anything gets done at all! This is not my intention. What I am trying to do is combat what I perceive to be an all-too-common attitude: that once you have decided what to do, doing it is straightforward. This is rarely true, at least in my experience, and I doubt it is ever true when it comes to managing complex organizational change which is the main subject of this section. So, even if the negativity puts you off a little, I would prefer that you approach these implementations with your eyes open and with the benefit of some serious preparation.

Project review

Most professional consulting firms include some kind of project review in their processes. This generally takes the form of an interview between a partner (or someone senior) in the consulting firm and the client. Occasionally the consulting team will take some time to review what they have learnt from the project and to look at what other opportunities there are with that client. It rarely goes further than this.

Perhaps this is not surprising: consulting projects tend to be quite intense and very focused on the objectives which have been set. When the objectives have been achieved, there is a sense of relief and a desire for closure. People go back to what they were doing before or move on to new tasks. There is very little appetite for *post-mortems* or for trawling through the whole project again.

Although such behaviour may be understandable, the consequence is that many of the potential benefits from the project are not realized, both for the client and for the consultant. This is a pity because there is usually quite a bit of value to be extracted.

Firstly, consulting projects generally turn up a lot of information about an organization which would not otherwise be touched. This information is viewed by people who are external to the organization and who (usually) have a broad range of other experience. Due to the focus on completing the project, a lot of the information is discarded as unnecessary to the objectives or simply not given any further thought. A project review phase is the ideal opportunity for the client to get the consultants and client team members together and collect their views about the organization as a whole, or about any particular pieces of information which may have struck them as significant but which did not fall within the immediate remit of the project. In this way, the information is at least captured. If the client chooses to, the process can be taken further and specific actions planned to follow up or investigate.

Secondly, each project teaches the participants about the consulting process. Capturing the key learning points from the project can help both the client and the consultant manage future projects more effectively. Some of these points will have been learnt subliminally by the individuals involved. It can be helpful to take a step back, think explicitly about what has been learnt and get it down in a form which can be shared and discussed by everyone involved. This is especially true if these learnings are unlikely to be needed for a while—it is surprising how quickly they can be forgotten.

Thirdly, the project review can be used to strengthen and deepen the relationship between the client and the consulting firm. It is an opportunity to provide mutual feedback and to assess where the two organizations work well together and where they do not. From this base, the status of the relationship can be assessed and opportunities for future co-operation discussed.

Ideally, then, the project review should cover the process, the outputs and the relationship, as well as providing mutual feedback at multiple levels. It should also present this information in a form that can be shared and used for any subsequent actions. This may sound daunting, but it need not be: if properly planned, a thorough review of even a fairly complex project can be carried out in two or three days and may well provide the best return on investment of the whole project.

In most cases you will not be able to assess the success or failure of a project in an initial project review—it will be too soon for the results to be known. So it is a good idea to schedule brief follow-ups for a relevant period into the future. This can provide very useful information for future consulting projects.

Conclusions on the consulting process

I have tried to make clear in this chapter that an overly simplified approach to hiring consultants (define requirements, select consultants, do the work) exposes the client to considerable and often unnecessary project risk. The process set out here is more complex and involves more steps, but better reflects the realities of a consulting engagement. It is up to you as the prospective client (and to some degree the consultant you select) to decide which steps in the process are critical for the success of your project. The discussions in this chapter should help with these decisions.

If you become proficient at managing this process and hone your understanding of how consultants work, you should substantially improve the effectiveness of consulting projects in your organization. But this is not the whole story. In fact, it is only the start. Consulting projects do not take place in a vacuum and consulting services can be provided in several formats other than projects. It is only by looking beyond the project, beyond the individual instances of the process described here, that you can really get the most out of consultants.

This broader view is the subject of the rest of this book. Whereas the first three chapters have looked at consultants and how they work, the chapters that follow will turn the lens back on the client organization and what it needs to do to make the most of the consultants it works with.

CHAPTER 4

The Size of the Prize

They say that 'you can't manage what you can't measure' (or, in another version, 'what gets measured gets done'). A lack of measurable data would go some way to explaining why organizations do not try to improve how they work with consultants. Large organizations typically have only the vaguest notion of how much they use consultants, what they pay and what they get for their money. At first I was surprised by this and not a little critical, but then I had a go at getting the information myself. Almost without exception, when I have tried to get a clear picture of consulting activities in an organization, I have quickly found myself in a minefield of obfuscation, political agendas, diverted budgets, re-labelled expenditures and plain ignorance.

Even in relatively transparent organizations in which information is readily available, trying to get a handle on the scope for improvement can be difficult—absolute measures like costs may not be too hard to find, but it is much more difficult to assess things such as consultant productivity and effectiveness, let alone your own productivity and effectiveness in working with consultants. And it doesn't end there—even if you can dig out metrics that you are happy with, you will probably have to persuade a number of other audiences that the metrics you propose are the right ones. If you are not careful, you will tie yourself into knots working out what you currently do before you even begin to think about how to improve it.

Nevertheless, some form of quantification is essential if you want to: know what you stand to gain; set and clarify your goals; justify any actions you wish to take; and then track how well you are carrying them out. The first of these, assessing what you stand to gain, is particularly important because the answer may turn out to be 'not much': for some organizations, simply developing a greater awareness of (and focus on) the things I have covered in the first three chapters will already bring significant improvement. And I would certainly recommend doing this first as it costs little or nothing to implement. The approach I describe in the chapters that follow, on the other hand, *will* cost something. How much will depend on what is already in place and what features you choose to implement. As with any investment, this is only worth doing if the benefits substantially outweigh the costs. So, in this context, that means that you should be able to identify significant potential beyond what can be achieved by simply improving your awareness.

For many organizations, the potential not only exists but is big enough to warrant some investment in achieving it. This chapter is about identifying and evaluating this potential. The first part of the chapter looks at how to build a picture of the consulting activities in your organization—what areas consultants are active in, how much they cost and how much value they bring. The second part explores, at a generic level, how consultants create value and key levers that clients can pull to influence this value. If you think about how this applies to your organization, you should be able to develop an order-of-magnitude assessment of what you stand to gain—the 'size of the prize'. It should also give you a first idea of what you have to do to achieve it and whether or not it is going to be worth the effort.

Armed with this information, you should be ready to think about how to structure an improvement initiative and where this should be focused. In the final part of this chapter, I outline what such an initiative might look like and suggest what its major components might be.

Understanding where you are today

The structure of this chapter follows the sequence of activities you will need to carry out in order to define your approach. The first of these is to gather information about what you do now. But before you get started on the data gathering and analysis outlined in this section, I would suggest that you read the rest of the chapter. Like all data-gathering exercises, this one will be both more efficient and effective with a clear view of what information is needed and how it is to be used. The subsequent sections explain and go into more detail on a number of the areas mentioned here, in particular the mechanics of value creation, and this should help you decide what you need from your data gathering.

What to look for ...

To begin building a picture of how your organization uses consultants you need to ask questions about (more or less in order of difficulty) cost, activity and value delivered. From these you can go on to get an idea of the productivity and effectiveness both of the consultants you work with, and of your organization in working with them.

Cost

- How much do you spend on consulting fees?

- How does this spend split out (by supplier, project, type of consulting, function, business unit, geography and any other category that is relevant to your organization)?
- How consistent is this spend? What variance do you see from year to year?
- How discretionary is the spend? If you didn't hire consultants to do the work, would you have to get someone else?
- How much do you spend on consultants as a proportion of your total costs, of your payroll costs and of your total consulting projects spend?
- Excluding the cost of the consultants, how much does your organization spend on working with consultants (e.g. cost of time spent on each step of the consulting process described in the previous chapter)?

Activity

- How many consulting man days were worked in the organization during the period you are looking at? How did this activity split out (as above)?
- How does the activity relate to cost in each category?
- How much of your employees' time was taken up by the consulting projects and who was affected? This should be linked back to cost.

Value

- How much value did the consultants bring? How does this split?
- Was value destroyed as a result of projects failing or because of disruption caused?

- Did any of the projects result in value destruction being avoided or reduced?
- Did they bring value beyond what could have been achieved by your own employees?
- How does the value delivered compare to the original objectives of the projects?
- What is the option value of your consultant relationships? What costs were avoided and opportunities exploited because you had the option to use consultants if the need arose?

Productivity (doing things right)

- How much value do your consultants bring in proportion to their cost? This should be assessed by type of consulting and may be broken down further. It may be possible to do some benchmarking here.
- How much value is created in proportion to the time and money invested in the consulting process?
- What is the relative productivity of the consulting projects you have run? How does this compare between the categories of project you have defined?
- Do you have any external benchmarks of consultant productivity? How do your projects compare?

Effectiveness (doing the right things)

- Were consultants used for the right things?
- Did you choose the right consultants?
- How effective were the methods the consultants employed?

Value, productivity and effectiveness can be extremely difficult to assess. I find that this difficulty is influenced most by the type of consulting you are looking at: when you hire consultants as a resource to do work that would otherwise be done by your own employees, the assessment is easier; it gets harder if the consultants are in a management role and even more difficult when they are providing analysis; and the most difficult types of work to assess are where consultants provide insight, such as strategic recommendations. The value of a strategy, if it is implemented, can be affected by many extraneous factors and may not become apparent for many years.

If I have laboured the difficulty of finding these metrics, it is not to discourage you from trying: as is often the case with measurement, it forces you to clarify your thinking. And even the process of looking for the numbers will improve your understanding of how consultants add (or destroy) value in your organization and may well suggest ways in which this could be improved. Just don't be disappointed if you don't have a nice set of fully reconciled figures at the end of it.

... And where to find it

In view of the difficulties I have mentioned above, I have found that it is helpful to approach the problem from as many directions as possible and to build up a picture project by project. This can be messy and so it helps to have an idea of how much detail you can realistically assemble in the time available. Once you have set this constraint, stick to it—the Pareto principle applies here and a really detailed understanding of every single consulting project is unnecessary.

Financial data

The most obvious starting point are the management accounts. These usually require some detective work because consulting costs can fall under various headings such as 'contractors', 'IT services', 'technical advice', 'professional fees' etc. This is particularly true of organizations where there have been restrictions placed on the hiring of consultants. Consulting costs will not necessarily appear in the Profit and Loss account (Income Statement): some projects are capitalized and the consulting costs are capitalized with them.

The management accounts often provide a reasonable starting point for looking at the costs of consulting projects. But it is important to be aware of their limitations: in many organizations, the management accounts are less than transparent; there are often consequent and contingent costs associated with projects that are not recorded as such; more generally, it is rarely clear what has been included and what has not; and most management accounts will give you little or no information about the value created.

Talking to the project teams

There is often a considerable amount of useful information that resides with the people who worked on a project, information that never makes it to the management accounts or other formal records. Some of this will be documented (progress updates, benefits tracking, project reviews etc.), but may not have been collated or made available for general use (i.e. it is sitting in boxes or in someone's bottom drawer). The best way to access this is to talk to the people involved.

Tackle the easy areas first: there tends to be more information on projects that are considered a great success or a total failure.

Everyone who employs consultants has pet projects or projects that they believe have been particularly successful. They will be happy to talk about these, sometimes at far greater length than you might want! At the other end of the spectrum, the unsuccessful projects may well have been the subject of some scrutiny to assess the causes of failure. Apart from the successes and failures, the more recent projects will be easier to get information on because they will be fresher in people's minds. You have to be quick though—most people's memory starts fading after a few weeks and less if they are busy on something else.

For the rest, I would suggest a two-pronged approach: top and bottom. The person who commissioned the project or the project director will have an overview of what happened and how it relates to what was going on in the organization at the time. This view may be biased, but it should provide useful context nevertheless. They will also be able to direct you to the people who were involved in the day-to-day running of the project. If you want to get any hard data, these are the people you will need to talk to.

The project director may refer you to the consultants as well. This can be useful because consultants often keep records such as time sheets that they do not automatically share with clients but that they would be willing (or obliged) to provide if asked.

Consultant proposals and reports

Where they are available, the consultants' proposals can be very useful: most proposals should present some idea of the benefits that were envisaged at the start of a project.

For many projects, there will also be some form of report summarizing the outputs of the project. For some projects, there may be interim reports too. These should give you some idea of what you are getting for your money and you can cross-check them (to some extent) against the proposal and the benefits actually achieved to get a more accurate view.

Other projects

A good number of the projects that involve consultants are not consultant-led and may not be classified as consulting projects. So it is worth running through the list of all projects your organization has been involved in (assuming you can pull one together) and checking whether they involved consultants.

This process can be greatly facilitated if your organization has a method for tracking projects. Where this is not the case, you may be able to work it out from purchase orders and invoices, but I have found that these frequently get misallocated —budget gets 'borrowed' from other areas or consultants working on projects end up spending some of their time on different projects and this never gets accounted for. You will need to make a judgement call on whether this is worth examining. In some organizations these practices are so pervasive that it is impossible to get an accurate picture of consulting activity in any other way.

Support functions

Discussions with the support functions in the organization can also be a helpful way of getting information. Finance, HR and, to some extent, IT tend to take a slightly different view of the organization than front-line functions; they often keep their own records; and they are likely to have been involved in any consulting assignments because they are generally one of the main sources of information for consultants working in the organization.

Given the legwork that is involved in finding this data and pulling it together, it may be tempting to use a consultant. I would caution against this. Every organization has its own system of information repositories and information flows. Someone who has some length of service with the organization is more likely to know how to tap these sources, will have their own network and is less likely to be treated with suspicion than someone brought in from the outside. If you are short of resources and must use consultants, get them to help with organizing the data collection, collating the data and carrying out the analysis. If you really have no choice but to use consultants to gather the data, keep them away from sensitive areas and try to get the consultants to pair up with insiders.

Assessing the potential benefits and defining the objectives

Interesting though all this information may be, it will do you no good unless you do something with it. So it is important not to get too involved in analysis for its own sake. The purpose of gathering the information is twofold: to identify (broadly) in what areas the organization can hope to benefit by getting better at working with consultants and to see how well these potential benefits fit with your general strategy and objectives. If the fit is poor, you may choose not to pursue the matter even though you know that you are leaving value on the table. If, on the other hand, the fit is good, you need to get a better idea of what is to be gained.

This section is about how you evaluate the potential benefits, from the most obvious (reducing consulting spend) to the more complex (organizational effectiveness in using consultants). Despite what I said at the start of this chapter, my main focus in this section will not be on quantification (although I have made a few points about it at the end of the section). There are three reasons for this: firstly, organizations differ greatly in the data they have available, the processes for collecting that data and the information that needs to be produced in order to justify an investment; secondly, any set of measures I propose would be more relevant to one organization than to another because the notion of value itself depends on the organization; and thirdly, if you have a good understanding of the mechanisms through which value is delivered and drivers of this value, you can usually work out some way (it really doesn't matter how crude) of measuring the value, whereas the reverse is not true. So, rather than focusing on ways of measuring, I shall focus on these mechanisms and value drivers and the actions you can take to influence them.

Reducing your consulting spend

The amount spent on consulting fees is the easiest consulting metric for an organization to produce. It is perhaps not surprising then that when clients set out to improve the value they get from consulting, the initial focus tends to be on cost. This usually comes in one of two flavours: what I call the 'nuclear option'— stopping all (or most) consulting activities— and a more measured approach that involves working the costs out over a period of time.

The nuclear option

The quickest way to save costs on consultants is to stop using them. Indeed, the flexibility to do this is one of the main benefits of using consultants in the first place. Some organizations do this on a fairly regular basis: investment banks, for instance, have been known to stop all consulting projects during a downturn and to start them again when business improves.

This approach can be counterproductive: if the projects which the consultants are working on are business critical, the removal of the consultants simply leads to increased workload for existing staff, the hiring of new staff or longer projects. In the first case, staff get distracted from other important obligations, the second leads to additional and not necessarily controllable costs and the third to an increased cost due to the sustained requirement for project overheads and to project completion and quality risks.

When a consulting project is interrupted with the intention of resuming later, the impact on total project costs and delivery risks is even more severe. Deferred costs do not diminish by virtue of being deferred and the costs of reviving a project that has been left dormant for a while can be high, often the same as starting from scratch.

An outright ban on consulting is only likely to be respected in an organization with a very strong central command and control culture. For organizations with less centralized structures, there is a danger that such a ban will be ignored or that the costs will simply be hidden in other budget codes. To these issues one must add the cost of policing the ban and of ensuring that headcounts do not rise as a result.

I am not saying that this kind of ban is necessarily a bad idea—as a short term cash flow remedy it can be extremely effective—but that it should be used with caution and with a full understanding of the consequences. Even then, it remains a drastic measure and should not be part of a medium to long term plan to manage consultants. For this, a more structured approach is required.

Medium-term cost reduction

A structured approach to reducing consulting costs, which avoids reducing the level of service (i.e. increases efficiency and productivity), takes a little more time and thought. The key is to understand why these costs are created and where they are unnecessary by examining:

- Projects that should never have happened
- Projects that failed to deliver
- Duplication
- Consolidation opportunities
- The alternatives to using consultants
- The fit between consulting projects and the consultants used
- Badly managed or inefficient projects
- The organizational costs of employing consultants
- Co-ordination of consulting work done for the organization in line with a consulting strategy

Projects that should never have happened are those that can bring little or no benefit to the organization or that are set up in such a way that they cannot succeed. As I have said before, consulting is bought for all kinds of reasons, many of which are not necessarily in the organizations overall interest. Managers buy consulting to provide a stamp of credibility, or because they feel insecure and want someone to share the blame if things go wrong, or because they feel that their superiors are more likely to believe the consultants than they are to believe them. Or it may be because they are subject to a headcount freeze and want to get certain work done, or because the consultants have done a particularly good sales job. A particularly bad case occurs when managers cannot make up their minds about something and just wheel in consultant after consultant to perform study after study until the problem is no longer relevant. One company I worked for commissioned no fewer than eight strategy projects in the space of two years and acted on the recommendations of none of them! Many more reasons could be added. Such projects should never have existed in the first place, but they can be difficult to eradicate because the personal motivations behind them are often strong. The issue can also be divisive—one person's unnecessary project is another person's business critical initiative.

Projects that have failed or will fail to deliver are important in two ways: as a potential saving and as an indicator of what is going wrong. It is surprising how often projects that have clearly failed are kept going under their own momentum, or because people have failed to realize or accept that circumstances have changed or in the hope that something will eventually come of them. Just going through and stopping these projects can reduce consulting costs by quite a bit, with little or no risk. Where projects have failed and been stopped, it is important to look at what has gone wrong (and by this I mean what *you* have done wrong, not the consultants) to prevent it happening again and to weed out the projects where it already is happening again.

Duplication is a common problem, especially in larger, more dispersed organizations. But it is not limited to such organizations—I have seen consultants engaged on the same remit by two different departments in the same building! Not only is duplication of projects a waste of money, but it can lead to misalignment problems when the results of the projects diverge.

Duplication of projects brings *opportunities for consolidation* and other projects can sometimes be consolidated too. Projects with similar objectives, or which share workstreams in common can be managed as a single project. You should take some care in assessing the benefits of this approach because it is not always suitable. The benefits lie in sharing project overheads, common workstreams and set-up costs. But this may be offset by higher co-ordination costs and a tendency to produce 'one size fits all' solutions which are not always the most appropriate or the best value for money.

Alternatives to consultants are rarely given enough attention. Where they are looked at, it is often as a straight choice between internal and external resources. And it is certainly true that consultants often end up doing 'day jobs' in organizations that have poor human resources management. But the choice is rarely binary. For any given task, there is a gamut of options to consider: many large organizations have internal consultants and other types of project or service groups which can respond to specific requirements faster and more affordably than external consultants; the market for interim managers is often overlooked or under-exploited; in some cases contractors are an option; or you might be able to bring in people the organization employs in other geographies and business units. I have even heard of teams with specific skills sets being brought in on loan from other organizations.

The fit between the consultants used and the tasks that they are required to carry out is another area where value is lost. Many consultants are not hired in the context of a 'consulting project', but to fill roles in internal projects which have become vacant or which the organization does not have the resources to fill. When I see a consultant from a top strategy firm sitting around on a client site running a project office, I cannot help feeling that the client is wasting their money. It is like using an expensive sports car to drive around town: it may look impressive, but it not good for your wallet or for the car. Conversely, using relatively inexpensive consultants on difficult projects that require experience and expertise is, to continue the motoring analogy, like entering a Formula One race with a family car—it may cost less, but it is a false economy because you have no chance of achieving a result.

Poorly managed consulting projects are quite common, but it is not always easy to remedy this once a project is underway. Nor is it necessarily easy to say which projects are well-managed and which are not, or which aspects of a project are well or poorly managed—this usually requires quite an involved understanding of the project in question. So, I would suggest that tinkering with live projects (unless they are going seriously wrong) is probably a bad idea and that this aspect of consultant cost reduction be reserved (mostly) for developing best practice in future projects.

The organizational cost of using consultants is often poorly understood and this cost can easily exceed the fees charged by the consultants. It is common for there to be substantial client teams involved in consulting projects and for many other employees to be affected directly or indirectly. On top of this there is the general level of disruption caused by a major project. One cannot hope to quantify these factors with any precision, but some idea of the role they play can be useful in planning how the organization should approach and prepare for such projects.

The inefficiencies described above should offer some scope for cost reduction in existing consulting activities. In my experience, such opportunities should be fairly easy to identify. To manage future consulting costs down, you will need to ensure that these inefficiencies do not recur. This requires more sustained monitoring of consulting activities, which is one of the topics of the next chapter.

Measurement baselines in cost reduction

To conclude this section on cost reduction, I should like to return to the question of measurement. I have found that a clear and broadly accepted baseline against which savings are measured is the foundation for any effective cost reduction programme. So I would like to devote a few lines to the issues to be considered here. This is a technical question and this section is aimed at practitioners, so those who are not interested are invited to skip this and go straight to the section on flexibility.

In most organizations, costs are controlled through the budgeting process: the previous year's actuals are examined and savings are identified for each budget code (there are, of course, other approaches, but this remains the most common). This process does not work very well for consulting because the consulting spend can vary hugely from one year to the next and from one part of the organization to another. So the only number from the previous year's actuals which is of relevance is the total consulting spend—because this is the number you are trying to reduce.

The problem with this is that the need for consultants tends to run in cycles. So it is entirely possible to achieve substantial savings against this number simply because there is less need for consulting in a given year. This is more a result of luck than judgement and only indirectly reflects genuine savings achieved through a cost reduction initiative.

One alternative is to target savings against budgeted figures (which already take into account the reduced need for consultants). Usually, though, only a relatively small part of the money spent on consulting is budgeted for specific, planned projects. Much consulting work arises as a result of urgent requirements and is paid for out of a general consulting fund, out of funds for other projects, or is 'stolen' from other budgets. These sources need to be taken into account if you want to avoid the costs being shunted around between budget codes.

Another alternative is to look at consulting costs over the longer term—three to five years—in the same way as one would look at an investment cycle. Where it is possible to take this approach, it effectively resolves the issue of year-on-year fluctuations and makes it much easier to manage consulting costs down. Unfortunately, most cost reduction programmes have much shorter time horizons.

Lastly, you could dispense with the baseline altogether and take a project-by-project approach, based on the lessons learned from a systematic review at the end of each project. Over time, the amount of waste (or value lost) discovered in the reviews should decrease. The downside of this approach is that there is no big round number to aim for (and build a business case around) or to wave in front of your sponsors once the cost reduction is completed.

Increasing your flexibility

'Flexibility' and 'nimbleness' have been buzzwords of management literature in recent years and staples of economic theory for much longer. The desire to be 'flexible' is a response to uncertainty: in a world where everything is known in advance, there is no need for flexibility or the costs that come with it. We do not live in such a world and the trend is towards ever greater uncertainty driven by the rapid (and unpredictable) advances in technology, globalization and an ever more complex geopolitical environment.

There are three generic approaches to dealing with uncertainty: insurance, focus and flexibility.

Insurance means that you build the capabilities to deal with all (or at least most) eventualities. It is most suitable when there are relatively few uncertainties to deal with and means that you are ready to seize the opportunity when the uncertainty is resolved. An example would be when there are two new technologies, you know only one of them will win, but you don't know which. The downside, clearly, is the cost—it means that you invest in capabilities that you will never need.

Focus is when you place all your eggs (or investment) in one basket. The value of this approach is that it is highly efficient. It is most appropriate where the uncertainty is peripheral to your main activity and where the downside of getting it wrong is limited. The problems with focus are that you are more exposed to 'unknown unknowns' and you are not in a position to exploit opportunities as uncertainties are resolved.

Flexibility is a compromise between the other two solutions. It is an option on capacity and capabilities that may or may not be needed. It means you can deal with negative events and exploit opportunities when they arise. But, like with a financial option, flexibility has a cost: maintaining the availability of flexible resources takes time and money, there is usually a set-up cost each time they are employed, they are more expensive than dedicated resources and, in some cases, they may not perform as well.

Most organizations will employ a mix of these strategies to deal with the plethora of uncertainties that they face. Using consultants is one way to create flexibility. The reason for introducing the other two strategies is that these are the alternatives you need to consider in evaluating the flexibility that consultants can provide. In assessing the value that consultants can bring, bear in mind that, by having a consulting relationship, you are avoiding the cost of the insurance approach and the risk of focus. So this flexibility has a value even if you don't actually use the consultants. How big this value is depends partly on the alternatives and partly on what you have done to optimize your flexibility. In order to do this, I find it useful to break this flexibility into three types: resource flexibility, reaction speed and geographical flexibility.

Resource flexibility

The resources in an organization can be divided into two groups: fixed and flexible (with varying levels of semi-flexible resources in between). Fixed resources are those which cannot be easily or quickly reallocated to other tasks, flexible ones can (but usually cost more because of this). Every organization has its own mix of resources depending on what types of activity it is involved in. With regard to people ('human' resources) flexibility is limited by skills and experience, by the number of people available and by the constraints contained in their employment contracts. Consultants can be used to provide additional flexibility in all three of these areas.

Reaction speed

In an uncertain environment, there is value in being able to react quickly when an uncertainty is resolved and creates an opportunity or a threat. Reaction speed is partly a function of resource flexibility. To react quickly an organization needs to have the structures in place to make decisions quickly and the processes to organize and mobilize resources rapidly. If you set things up right, consultants can be an important part of this response because they excel at setting up teams to tackle urgent issues quickly.

Geographical flexibility

Geographical flexibility needs little explanation. As organizations continue to expand across borders, it is imperative to have partners who are already in place and who have the local knowledge to evaluate and facilitate activities where the organization does not yet have a presence. Accountants, lawyers and chambers of commerce can help with the technicalities, but consultants are better placed to help on the organizational and business sides.

So how can an organization use consultants to achieve its desired level of flexibility? There are two broad objectives:

- To ensure that the right resources are available at short notice where they are required
- To ensure that these resources can be mobilized rapidly

To achieve these objectives, you need to

- Develop and maintain a network of consultants covering the range of capabilities that are likely to be needed
- Inform the relevant individuals about the relationships that exist
- Streamline commissioning procedures
- Initiate and maintain a dialogue with suppliers to ensure that they are aware of potential requirements as early as possible (ideally before they are fully defined) and can plan their resources accordingly.
- Develop common project set-up procedures so that less time is wasted getting a project going. This is particularly useful where consultants are used frequently for time-critical projects.

None of these actions is particularly complex, but they do take considerable effort to set up and maintain. The cost of this effort needs to be set against the flexibility it provides and, more importantly, what this flexibility is worth to you.

To change the level of flexibility, it helps to have a way of quantifying it. The most effective method I have found is to develop a set of scenarios for events which would require the use of flexible resources. You can then assess your organization's readiness to respond in these scenarios against your chosen performance metrics. Apart from providing a scoring system for organizational flexibility, this approach has the added benefit of giving some idea of the extent to which a given scenario can be dealt with internally and what the requirement is likely to be for external resources. This method is not perfect—you need to be very careful in defining your scenarios to genuinely test flexibility and there is a tendency to be optimistic in assessing one's ability to respond—but it is the best method I have found.

So, working with consultants can provide considerable tactical flexibility for an organization (strategic flexibility is more fundamental and stems from the organization's strategy and design). Most organizations, without even knowing it, derive some value from the fact that they can call in consultants when needed. But this value can, in many cases, be greatly enhanced by taking a careful look at the flexibility that is likely to be required and setting things up in advance so that consultant interventions can be as efficient and effective as possible.

Consultant productivity and organizational receptiveness

You can achieve lower costs and higher flexibility by varying the amount of consulting that is used, by choosing consulting suppliers and what they are used for more astutely, and by structuring relationships with these suppliers. These are broad measures that can be run as a central initiative. But if you want to improve the efficiency and effectiveness of the consultants you work with, you need to roll up your sleeves and take a close look at how consulting projects are managed and how well the organization itself is adapted to working with consultants and getting the maximum value from these projects.

Consultant productivity simply means that you get more value for each dollar you spend on consulting. It is important to understand that 'value' does not necessarily equate to 'work': consultants deliver value (or fail to) as much through their expertise and their ability to communicate, influence, mobilize or mollify people in the organization as they do by carrying out specific tasks. Some of the best consultants I have seen have been able to make a huge difference to their clients with a relatively small time input. So looking at the hours worked against the fees paid (which is all that some organizations do) will not even come close to giving you an idea of consultant productivity.

In most organizations consultant productivity is more a matter of luck than good process: if the organization happens to hire a good consulting team, they get high consultant productivity; if they do not, they don't. Choosing the right team is easier when the organization uses consultants regularly, because you can have some input into the composition of the team and have some experience of the individuals involved. But hiring the same team again for a different project is no guarantee of success—teams must be tailored for the project.

To do this you need to get to know your consultants. This does not just mean knowing the consulting firms you work with, but the individual consultants that have worked for the organization (and possibly some that have not). In exchange for this effort, you get much better team selection, but only if the information is available and accessible to those who are involved in commissioning the projects.

Project startup costs are another area where consultant productivity can usually be improved. Every time a project starts, consultants must set up the project management structure and procedures, they must familiarize themselves with the organization, develop or reactivate their network of contacts within the organization and build a team to carry out the project. Streamlining this process through pre-agreed structures and procedures, consultant 'information packs', regular contacts with individual consultants (even when no project is running) and an accelerated team-building process can yield benefits that can add up to a significant percentage of the project cost.

It is not only the project teams (clients and consultants) who need to be prepared—all those commissioning and overseeing consulting projects and, to some extent, the organization as a whole need to be ready too. Employees are often uncertain how to react to a consulting team in their midst and it takes some time and effort before they are sufficiently comfortable to work with them effectively.

While consultant productivity can be enhanced by careful selection, preparation and good management, the single greatest creator and destroyer of value in consulting is not the consultant but the client organization. Specifically, I am referring to the organization's capabilities in working with consultants, in absorbing the outputs of the consultants' work and in minimising the disruption caused by consulting projects.

I cannot stress this point enough and it is at the heart of the approach described in this book: many organizations use consultants in the same way as they use powerful computers—for word processing. I have yet to encounter an organization that has taken a serious look at how it is set up to work with consultants. For this reason, if for no other, there is usually a substantial reservoir of untapped value in this area and I would venture to speculate that in many organizations the benefits from improving receptiveness are greater than all the other areas combined.

Of course, the benefits from improved consultant productivity and organizational receptiveness are the most difficult to quantify and to achieve. This may be one of the reasons why they are rarely addressed. I have struggled with this on several occasions and have developed quite complex quantification models. With the benefit of hindsight, I think much of this work was a waste of time (although it did provide some valuable insights). Now I favour a simpler approach: to poll the key buyers of consulting on a regular basis about a set of indicators that have been selected to track the areas where the organization needs to improve. This may not give an accurate, objective picture, but it will at least give a directional indication of whether things are improving or deteriorating and by how much. This should be quite sufficient to steer the initiative.

The final point I would like to make about the benefits assessment is that there can be ancillary benefits to developing your consultant management capability. I shall discuss these benefits in more detail in the final chapter, but it is worth mentioning here that these ancillary benefits can add to and even outstrip the benefits which can be achieved through consultant management alone. Where this is the case, the initiative to improve consultant management can be used as a catalyst for much broader organizational change.

Deciding what to do

It is only worth managing consultants better if it brings sufficient value to warrant the effort and the inevitable disruption this causes. But this is not a simple 'yes' or 'no' decision—it is entirely reasonable (and usually necessary) to take some of the benefits and incur only some of the costs and disruption, or to phase the development of your capabilities to fit in with your organization's other priorities.

Context too is important: if the objective is to reduce costs and consulting accounts for one per cent of controllable costs, then you are probably better off focusing your efforts elsewhere.

If you have carried out your value assessment and come to the conclusion that there is an opportunity worth exploiting, the natural question to ask is 'what should we do now?' My answer to this question, the approach to working with consultants that I propose, is comprised of four main components:

- Building and managing your consulting *knowledge*
- Developing the capabilities you will need to work more effectively with consultants through *learning*
- Co-ordinating the projects in your consulting *portfolio*
- Cultivating your consulting *relationships*

I refer to these components as the 'consulting mix'. As with a marketing mix or a product mix, these elements should reinforce each other and the key to an effective consultant management strategy is to balance them in a way that supports your organization's objectives. The process of balancing these components—of 'configuring' the mix—is discussed in Chapter 9. But before we get into this, the next four chapters take a closer look at each of the four components individually.

CHAPTER 5

Managing What You Know About Consultants

If you have followed the suggestions in the previous chapter, you will have built up a picture of how your organization works with consultants, what it stands to gain by doing this better and how much time and money you might be prepared to invest in achieving this improvement. You may also have some idea of how long this might take, or at least how long you want it to take. Now you need to decide what you are actually going to do and where you should start.

There are several ways you can approach this, depending on where you perceive your areas of strength and weakness to be. You may feel, for instance, that your work with consultants is insufficiently co-ordinated and opt to focus on developing a more active management of your consulting portfolio. Or you may take the view that your relationship with consultants is too transactional and that there is value to be gained from having more frequent and less project-specific interactions, in which case you would want to put some effort into relationship development. But I would suggest that you start by building up your organization's knowledge of consultants and how to work with them. In most organizations that I have looked at, this is the most important driver of consultant value. Knowledge gives you more control, promotes better decision-making, saves time, helps prevent wasted effort, increases flexibility and underpins just about any other action you may choose to take.

It is worth noting that for many organizations there is a significant imbalance between what they know about consultants and what the consultants know about them. Most consulting firms that you work with (and some you do not work with) will have detailed files about your organization: not just organizational charts and financial statements, but analysis of issues, challenges, strengths, weaknesses; competitive assessments; profiles of individual managers and their preferences and issues; influence maps showing who relates to whom and how. And you can be pretty certain that most consultants working for you will have been well briefed on all of this information and will have gone to some effort to talk to other consultants who have worked for you. To some extent, this is to be expected and is in the client's interest—consultants usually need to know about your organization to do their job—but there does come a point when the imbalance between what they know about you and what you know about them becomes detrimental: it may put you at a commercial disadvantage when negotiating consulting contracts or allow consultants power and influence that they can use in their interests rather than yours. So, if you want to get better at working with consultants, you need to improve your organization's knowledge about consultants and consulting.

To achieve this, it helps to have some clarity on what 'knowledge' is. The first point to make here is that knowledge is not synonymous with information. For some readers, this point may seem obvious. 'Knowledge management' has been fashionable in the business world for a number of years now and for some organizations it is already a way of life. But the old attitude to knowledge, that it is information that can be captured, codified, stored and retrieved, is still pervasive. It is also extremely limiting—a bit like saying that you know how to drive a car because you own the manual.

Information is only knowledge to the extent that it can be applied and many aspects of knowledge are not easy to pin down. These are what is known as 'tacit' knowledge: the instinct we develop from experience; or the facility we gain from practice; the insights we gain from bringing together different points of view; the understanding of a situation that comes from having spent time with the individuals involved; or the cohesion we get from the shared experience, ideas and practice that can loosely be grouped under the umbrella of 'organizational culture'.

Although the advent of knowledge management has led to such tacit knowledge receiving more attention, the bias is still heavily towards explicit knowledge. The reason for this is simply that explicit knowledge is much easier to manage and control than tacit knowledge. When it comes to working with consultants, it is often in the tacit knowledge and the transfer of knowledge from tacit to explicit and back again that the value lies. My working definition is quite broad:

- It is the sum of know-how, know-what and know-who, know-when, know-why and know-where about consultants that is sitting in the heads of the people in your organization or is otherwise available for your organization to use.
- It is a collection of documents (electronic or hard copy) and databases with information about consulting firms, consultants, the consulting market and consulting projects together with the systems that cross reference these.

- It is a set of knowledge packs and other synthesized material that distil what the organization knows about particular consulting issues so that anyone can be brought up to speed on them quickly.
- It is a corporate directory or 'yellow pages' that enables people to get information or advice quickly by finding the people who know.
- It is the set of behaviours and processes that provide an environment where new knowledge is generated, shared, assimilated and applied. This would include, for instance, project and supplier reviews, training, policies and procedures, communities of practice and 'peer assists'.
- It is the systems that are used to capture, store, share, communicate and facilitate the creation of this knowledge, including intranets, extranets, virtual repositories, subject-specific chat rooms, bulletin-boards and virtual communities, and organizational wikis.

This is a generic definition. I have found it is not bad as a starting point, but is too abstract to use as a basis for a consulting knowledge management programme. For that you will need to refine it based on how it relates to your organization (structure, people, processes, culture, and systems) and to the way you intend to manage your consulting knowledge.

Given how intangible and fluid knowledge can be, it is legitimate to ask whether managing it is a realistic proposition and, given the effort involved, whether it is worth doing just for a 'non-core' activity like consulting.

My answer to the first question, whether it is worth managing knowledge, is an unequivocal 'yes'. Equipping a broad base of people with the essential information and skills for working with consultants can bring substantial benefits quickly. It is an approach employed, amongst others, by the military and lends itself well to a structured programme. It can be a particularly effective way to make the most of what you have if you are not starting off with an extensive consulting knowledge base. For more advanced or more specialized knowledge and where you want to encourage the creation of new knowledge, formal management tends to be less effective. Here it is less about programmes, objectives and plans and more about guidance, facilitation and support. This is a more subtle form of management, but it is management all the same.

As to whether or not it is worth setting up knowledge management specifically for consulting knowledge, the answer is a little less straightforward. Knowledge management can certainly help you work better with consultants. That, to my mind, is not in doubt. And it is usually possible to find a level of investment that does not involve over-commitment and gives satisfactory returns. The issue is that, in many cases, this return would be much higher if you did not limit your knowledge management efforts to consulting. If you already have a knowledge management programme in place, integrating your consulting knowledge into this is almost a no-brainer—it would cost next to nothing and should provide substantial value. If you do not have a programme in place and you are thinking of introducing one for consulting, you should at least consider applying it to a broader area of your activity. It may cost a bit more at the outset, but in most cases it will be well worth it.

Finding a knowledge management approach that suits you

Although any approach to knowledge management should touch upon all the elements I have included in the definition of knowledge, the emphasis and the way they are combined will naturally depend on the specifics of your organization. I cannot provide a universal approach to managing consulting knowledge because none exists, but I can suggest some of the things you should look at in deciding what is appropriate for your organization. I find it helps to focus your assessment around four areas:

- How much, how and in what circumstances you work with consultants currently
- Your consulting objectives in terms of the above parameters and what you are prepared to do or spend to achieve them
- The nature of the consulting knowledge that already exists in your organization and how this is managed
- Your organizational context, particularly with regard to how your organization interacts with consultants and the extent to which knowledge management disciplines are already established

The role of knowledge management in your consulting programme

If you look at your consulting objectives and set these against what you do today, you begin to get a picture of what needs to be done to achieve those objectives. As there are many variables and many more possible courses of action, this process can often be quite messy, but one thing that should come out of it is some idea of the role that knowledge and knowledge management are likely to play and, crucially, how much and what you are prepared to invest in it. This may not be a very precise number, but it should at least give you an idea of relative investment. It is essential to keep these objectives and constraints in mind when designing your knowledge initiative because it is very easy for such initiatives to become bloated. Knowledge may be limitless, but the time and resources available to harness it are not. So you need to define the limits and focus your efforts to stay within them. Keep in mind, though, that a certain amount of redundancy is necessary—you cannot always know in advance what knowledge you are going to need to develop or if a piece of knowledge is going to be valuable.

Focusing your knowledge management effort where it counts

In the same way as you assessed the gap between your existing consulting activities and your consulting objectives to determine the role that knowledge management is likely to play in your approach to consulting, the state of your existing consulting knowledge must be set against these same objectives if you are to focus your knowledge management efforts.

The complication here is that assessing your knowledge can be quite hard to do. The slightly abstract question of how you can know what you do not know is usually quite easy to deal with in practice and so I shall not dwell on it here. More problematic is the fact that there is no simple way to measure how much knowledge you have: is it about what you know? How well you know it? Who knows it? How many people know it? How quickly it is updated?... So you could, if pressed, score your consulting knowledge out of ten, but what would that actually tell you?

A comprehensive approach to this issue would be to build up a 'knowledge map' of your organization showing what is known where and how well. So, for instance, you would be able to see how many people have experience of working with marketing consultants or, more specifically, who has worked with a particular consulting firm to launch a new product in South America, how many times and in what capacity. Clearly, this mapping process can get cumbersome pretty quickly!

Fortunately, a complete knowledge map is not necessary (or desirable) at the outset. I suggest you look again at the areas where you think consulting is going to bring you the most value and then identify any knowledge shortfalls in these. This should be as specific as possible: what type of knowledge is lacking (e.g. data, analysis, contacts, experience, synthesis…)? Is it not available in the organization or is it simply not widespread enough? Is it something that can be bought in or do you have to learn it yourself? In the latter case, are the mechanisms in place for this learning to happen? When does it need to be in place?

If you can define a few knowledge targets like this, it should give you a kernel around which to build your consulting knowledge management. Bear in mind, though, that this is only the starting point and you are likely to discover more areas in which you want to improve your knowledge as you move forward.

Adapting your approach to your organizational context

The last area to consider in developing your approach is your organizational context, both in terms of how your organization relates to consultants and how it views knowledge. On the consulting side, you need to look at the attitudes to consulting that exist in your organization. This is key to understanding how much resistance you are likely to encounter in building your consulting knowledge. Some organizations are culturally opposed to the use of consultants and this can easily translate into opposition to learning more about them—'if we're not going to work with them, why should we learn about them?' Perversely, these attitudes can be found in organizations that use consultants quite extensively. Where this is the case, you will need to tackle the cultural issues before you can really get started on a consulting knowledge management programme and this will probably take some time. Alternatively, you could look at slipping consulting knowledge in through the back door by including it in a more general knowledge management programme and trying to change attitudes through this.

Where there is no cultural bias against consultants, you are still likely to encounter pockets of resistance, particularly where individuals have had bad experiences with consultants. Your approach to this will need to be case-specific: sometimes you can persuade such individuals that their bad experience may not have occurred if they had known a bit more and that developing the organization's consulting knowledge is the best way to prevent it happening again. Often, though, this sort of opposition can be more visceral than rational and you will have to plan your approach in such a way as to insulate your knowledge management programme (and, indeed, the whole of your consulting programme) from the individuals in question, at least until it has gained sufficient momentum. The one thing you should not do is ignore these people and hope they will go away.

The knowledge context of your organization will form the background against which your consulting knowledge management programme will take place. Here you need to look at biases about knowledge and learning and again these may be at the level of the organization as a whole, specific groups or just individuals. Some of the questions you might look at are:

- Does more emphasis get placed on what you know or on who you know?
- Is experience valued more or is it formal training and certification?

- Is there an organizational learning style and are individual learning styles likely to affect what you do?
- How consistent are these practices and preferences?
- What role does knowledge currently play in your organization? What has already been established?

Once you have an idea of how your organization approaches knowledge, you will need to decide whether to play to your strengths or develop the areas where you think you are weak.

Apart from the more general knowledge context of your organization, it is worth taking a look at people's perception of how much they know about consultants (and how much they need to know). This is a separate issue to their attitude to consultants which I discussed above. In fact, it is often in the organizations that are most pro-consulting that the need for knowledge is felt the least. Sometimes this is because there is genuinely a high level of consulting knowledge. More often it is a result of complacency. The aggregate level of this perceived need for consulting knowledge determines whether you adopt a 'push' or a 'pull' approach in your knowledge management. My own preference, where possible, is to apply a 'pull' or 'seeding' approach. Here the centralized activity is restrained and low profile. You aim to plant a few 'seeds' in the areas of the organization where there is the greatest perceived need and then focus your efforts on providing support and occasional guidance for the users to develop knowledge management in the direction that they feel will be most helpful. This is not generally a very fast approach, but it is inexpensive and has, to my mind, the great merit that users end up with what they feel they need (and so will use).

Unfortunately, a pull approach only works when there are sufficient users who perceive a need for consulting knowledge to generate the pull. Where this is not the case, a 'push' or 'kick start' approach is required. Here, there is a more substantial central investment at the outset, aimed at collecting and collating the needed material and putting in place the tools and procedures for it to be used. When it works, this can provide the necessary impetus to get things moving. My issues with it are, firstly, that it is not the users who are deciding what knowledge is important (even when you ask them) and, if you get it wrong, it will simply be ignored; secondly, that it can often take considerably more effort than initially envisaged to get the kick start effect; and thirdly, once things are up and running, it can be very difficult for the central, 'specialized' team to let go and hand control over to the users.

Finally, the knowledge management context will influence your approach in that you should try to leverage whatever knowledge management capabilities you already have. Most organizations manage knowledge in some way, even if the role sits under different organizational headings. Where a fully-fledged knowledge management capability is in place, it should be fairly easy to slot consulting knowledge into this. Where it is not, you can either develop it from scratch or cobble something together from what already exists in the way of databases, intranets, training programmes etc. Either approach can work in the right context. If you are completely new to knowledge management I would suggest preparing the organization a little before you launch into data gathering and collation—I find that time spent getting the idea of knowledge management across before you get into the mechanics is rarely wasted.

Working through the different considerations described above will give you the elements of a plan for managing consulting knowledge in your organization: the role that knowledge management is likely to play in your consulting programme; the aspects of knowledge management you want to focus on; and some idea of how to introduce it in the context of your organization. Once you have these elements, I would not recommend that you spend too long on detailed planning. I find, when I try to do this, that I usually need to have done the work to be able to plan it in detail, which rather defeats the object. For most organizations a few hours of thinking through who will do what is quite sufficient at this stage.

So, in keeping with my own advice, I shall leave planning now and move on to discuss what you actually need to do. In the remainder of this chapter I will focus on capturing what you know about consultants and making it available to the organization—creating a 'consulting knowledge base'. The next chapter will look at how you can develop your consulting knowledge both in terms of depth (what you know) and breadth (the number of people who know it). In other words, it is about how your organization can learn how to work with consultants.

My main reason for presenting things in this order is that many organizations (most, I suspect) already have a lot of knowledge about consultants that they can tap into. So, an initial focus on knowledge capture will help you assess, organize and begin to apply what you already have. That said, unlike books, organizations are not limited by the constraints of linearity and you may be better off doing a little in all areas, rather than taking one at a time. The broad aim should be to create a dynamic in which knowledge is created, captured, distributed and, above all, applied.

Building a consulting knowledge base

Before you go out and start building your knowledge base, be clear about the purpose it will serve. I appreciate that this may sound a little bland, so I should explain that, when I refer to clarity of purpose, I do not mean some vague statement of objectives but a fairly rigorous analysis. If your knowledge base is to bring value, it is worth being explicit about the mechanisms through which that value is to be delivered. It is all too easy to start doing things because you think they will bring value, without actually forcing yourself to understand how that value is generated. All too often, that value then evaporates. So a little rigour at this stage can save considerable embarrassment later.

A knowledge base works by capturing, structuring, making accessible and indexing the knowledge you have in your organization. And the existence of the knowledge base lets people know that the knowledge is there. This can increase the value of this knowledge in several different ways: knowledge capture makes it less likely that it will simply walk out the door as people leave your organization or change roles; having a formal knowledge capture process also increases the likelihood that the knowledge will be created in the first place because it gives people an incentive to think about and formulate what they have learnt; linking, indexing and cross-referencing make the knowledge more available to the individuals who need it, help ensure that you do not have to keep re-learning the same lessons and give you a solid foundation on which to build new knowledge; analysis, synthesis and other forms of preprocessing enable people to home in on what is important much faster, to benefit from collective wisdom and to use the knowledge more effectively. All the above is generic but should serve as a starting point. You should make it specific by spelling out precisely (with numbers, if possible) how you think these mechanisms are going to work in your organization and further your consulting objectives: it will help you focus your efforts, justify any investment and, further down the road, work out what is going wrong if you are not getting the results you expected.

Even when you are clear on how it will bring value, there will be many questions to answer and trade-offs to be made in designing your knowledge base. For instance: how much of your effort should go into collecting knowledge, how much into organizing and processing it and how much into making it available? Should you collect what you find in one place or should you simply map it so others know where to find it? Should you do anything with what you find or just leave it in its raw form? How should the knowledge be stored and who should have access to it?

It will come as a disappointment to some (and a relief to others!) that I am not going to answer these questions here: there are at least as many answers here as there are organizations to which you apply them; many of these issues are not specific to knowledge management or consulting; and to attempt a full answer would take me too far off topic and into the rather detailed, technical territory that would probably not be suitable for most readers of this book. Make no mistake, though, this detail is at least as important to achieving your goals as the higher-level strategic thinking. So, if detail is not your bag, make sure you have someone on your team whose bag it is.

Rather than drown you in the detail, my aim in what follows is to start you off with some suggestions about what could go into your knowledge base and then to discuss two issues that I consider particularly important: the role of the users and keeping control of the knowledge base once it has gained momentum.

The contents of your knowledge base

When you set out to build a knowledge base, usually the first question that comes up is 'what should we put in it?' I shall discuss later why this may not be the best starting point, but given that it is so common, I have provided a 'shopping list' of things that might be included. It is worth saying up front that this is only intended to prompt your thinking. It contains items that may not be relevant to your organization and probably omits many that are. So please take it for what it is.

Information about the consulting market

- Overall size of market and relevant sub-markets
- Qualitative and quantitative trends in supply and demand
- Lists of consulting firms by number of professionals and by revenues
- Segmentation based on specializations and geographies
- Consulting stars—highly successful specialized teams (these may be separate firms or practices within larger firms)
- Innovations and trends in consulting practices and service offerings
- Indicative fee rates classed by level of experience and specialization

Information about consulting firms

- How is the consulting firm structured and who are the key people?

- What clients is the firm working for and who have they worked for in the past?
- What types of work have they done and with what level of success?
- How many people do they employ and how are these people distributed by activity and geography?
- What are the firm's relative strengths and weaknesses (both for the firm as a whole and for individual practices)?
- What are the firm's ambitions and development goals?
- What work have they done for your organization and how did it go?
- Who have they worked with in your organization?
- How are they perceived in your organization and in the market?
- What are their fee rates, classed by level of experience and specialization?
- What are their charging structures?
- What is their cost structure and business model?
- What is their operating model?
- What is their culture? What set of values do they work to?
- How do they recruit? What is the profile of their new recruits, at what stage in their careers are they recruited and what career paths do they typically follow?
- What points of contact, direct and indirect (e.g. through customers or suppliers), formal and informal exist between the firm and your organization?

Relationship and performance information about firms that you have worked with

- How many projects and of what size and type have they worked on?

- How long have you had a relationship and what is the history of that relationship?
- Which individual consultants have worked with you and how well do they know your organization?
- How well does the firm as a whole know your organization and which parts does it know best?
- How much have you spent on the firm (per year, total over relationship, for specific projects)?
- How did the results measure up to what was proposed?

Information about individual consultants (mostly those who have worked with you or your partners)

- Résumés that cover career history, projects they have worked on and areas of expertise.
- Assessment of each consultant who has worked in the organization by the individuals who have worked with them
- Inventory of work done for your organization and any others that may be sharing information with you
- Touchpoints: who has worked with each consultant, in what capacity and on what kind of project?
- Which employees have been consultants themselves?
- Have such employees been fully debriefed about their consulting experience and what is done with this material?
- A database of consulting projects, searchable by supplier, employee, type of work, date, geography etc.
- Names of people and groups (including contact details) who have developed expertise in particular aspects of consulting or particular types of consulting project

- A repository and index of all procedures and training materials relating to consultants
- Any proposals or plans for new material and the status of such material as it is created
- Database of individuals who have undergone training on working with consultants or who have been trained by consultants in specific areas

Work in progress and relevant changes

- Information about all current projects in the organization (except the top secret ones)
- Changes in consulting firms you are tracking (e.g. key new hires and departures)
- Tracking of consulting knowledge and learning goals
- Work being undertaken by communities of practice (see next chapter)

Analysis, synthesis and resource packs

- Comparisons of different consulting suppliers
- Assessments of consulting products
- 'Best practice' and 'quick start' packs along with their situational variants
- Operational guidelines for different roles

All roads lead to the user

Looking through my 'shopping list' above (and assuming you have decided to build a knowledge base), you might be asking yourself 'How do I decide which information is most relevant to me and will have the greatest impact on how we work with consultants?'

Or, if you are in project manager mode, 'What should my roll-out schedule look like and where should I allocate resources?' Or again, if you have a tidy mind, 'How should I structure all this information so that it is most useful and accessible?'

These are all good questions and there are long and fairly complex answers I could give to them. But there is only one answer that really matters and that can be stated in four words: FOCUS ON THE USERS. If you pay enough attention to who the users are and how they will use the knowledge base, the answers to these questions will come out of this. If you do not pay enough attention, then the answers to these questions will not matter because your knowledge base will not get used enough to make a difference. And usage is the only thing that really matters.

Why? Because a consulting knowledge base is not an academic exercise (unless, of course, you are an academic). It brings value by improving the quality of consulting decisions and by improving the efficiency and effectiveness with which consulting resources are applied. In short, to be valuable it must be useful. For it to be useful at the organizational level you have to use it. The more you use it, the more useful, and therefore valuable, it becomes. Of course, it is even more useful if you use it well, but this comes a distant second (from a value perspective) to how much you use it.

I expect some readers will not agree with this, so I should explain:

At the most superficial level, it is clear that the less a knowledge base is used, the lower the potential benefits and the lower the potential return on the effort made to create it. But it goes further than this—the less the knowledge base is used, the more out of date it becomes (because there is no immediate need to update it), the lower people's awareness of its contents and applications, and, eventually, the fewer people use it. Below a certain level of usage, any knowledge base is destined for terminal decline. A frequently used knowledge base, on the other hand, benefits from the opposite dynamic.

These dynamics can be powerful; so much so that I have seen cases where use of the knowledge base is mandated in order to promote a positive dynamic. Unfortunately, this does not work either—if people are using it because they have to and not because they perceive that it has something that will benefit them, it becomes a bureaucratic exercise and brings little value. The only scenario where mandatory use can work is where you are trying to kick start a new process and you need to shift people out of an old way of doing things into a new one. Even then, it has to catch on pretty quickly if it is going to stick.

In the long term, people will only use the knowledge base if they believe it will help them deal with specific problems that they expect to encounter when they work with consultants. This may seem simple to achieve, but quite a few elements have to be balanced for it to work well: you have to define the right users (i.e. the ones who will actually use the knowledge base and not the ones you think should!); you have to find out what content they think they want; then you have to work out what they are likely to use, how to get it, how best to deliver it to them and how to make them aware that it is there. The potential to get it wrong here is very high, especially if this is a centrally-driven, 'push' initiative. Here is a story to illustrate what I mean:

Early in my consulting career I was working for a mid-sized international firm. I had a bit of time between clients and my bosses decided that it would be a good idea to pull together what we knew about other consulting firms and the consulting market—I don't think the term 'knowledge base' had been coined at that point in time. As we were a consulting firm, this was a competitor database and its intended use was to give senior managers information about the competition when they were pitching for new work.

So I went ahead and interviewed a number of these senior managers to find out what they would find useful and then spent a fair bit of time pulling this information together from various internal and external sources (this was long before anything was online). I indexed all this information and placed it on a central server so that anyone with access to our network and the right permissions could use it. I then followed up by showing the intended users where the information was and how to access it. I also spent a few minutes with each of them explaining how it was structured and the way the index worked. The feedback I received was broadly positive and some users were even quite enthusiastic.

It was never used. Not once.

Needless to say, when I found out about this I was disappointed and not a little puzzled. I had, after all, gone to some effort to ensure that the users got precisely what they wanted. So I did a little digging to find out why the people who had asked me to put this together in the first place and who had seemed so enthusiastic about the result never used it. Here is what I found out:

Users can rarely explain what they want, let alone what they will actually use. What I thought had been pretty clear specifications turned out not to be. Most of the people I talked to had given me quite vague descriptions of what they wanted, but some had given me lengthy shopping lists (not unlike the one I have included in the previous section). I then took these more detailed lists and combined them into a master which I used for the data collection. The problem with this was that, out of all this information, there was only a small part that was actually valuable to the users. The rest was padding, or stuff that they thought it would be good to collect, but that did not serve any specific purpose. And the useful material was (in retrospect unsurprisingly) precisely the stuff that was unique to each user and that had mostly been left out in the process of aggregation. The users had not been specific enough in defining what was actually valuable to them and I had not looked hard enough at the value delivery mechanisms. If I had spent more time assessing how they were going to use it (rather than just asking them what they wanted) I would have either come up with a solution that was more integrated into their processes or I would have discovered that a global solution was not in fact possible because the requirements of individual users were incompatible.

There was no real knowledge transfer. The idea had been to pool everyone's knowledge about the competition so that we could learn from each other. The problem was that the people who knew the most in each area were both the sources of the information and the people who were supposed to be using it. Of course, someone in the US could look up what we knew about a particular competitor's operations in Japan, but in reality they were far more interested in what that competitor did in the US for the particular clients that they were targeting. And they knew this already. This issue was compounded by the fact that, where people did want to step out of the area they were familiar with, the information I had captured was too superficial to be useful. To use the same example, if the manager in the US had needed to find out about the competitor in Japan, they would simply have phoned the Japanese office. This is what they had always done and this is what they continued to do. So, for this kind of information, a corporate yellow pages would have been considerably more useful.

We had defined the wrong users. In hindsight, I think that, even if I had got it right, there was really very little value to be gained from doing this exercise for the users we were targeting.

We would have been better off focusing our global competitor knowledge on areas where it would bring more value such as service development or global account management. In these areas there would also be a chance that the information would be used often enough for it to be kept current. Infrequent use is particularly problematic with a consulting knowledge base because there is a tendency to view it as a support tool for buyers of consulting (which, of course, it is). Unfortunately, any given buyer of consulting is unlikely to buy with sufficient frequency to warrant their involvement in keeping the knowledge base current, let alone developing it further. So it is important to define a broader user base (and a wider variety of use cases) to maintain the momentum.

If I were given the same task today, I would (bosses permitting) spend considerably more time looking at who was going to use the information and how; and I would test my conclusions at each step by making these users walk through simulations of how they were to use it. Even then, it is much easier to get things right in hindsight than in reality and I could give other examples where these lessons were applied and things still did not turn out as expected—there are a lot of elements that have to be balanced for this to work. This is why a centralized approach such as I have described above is inherently risky and why a user-driven approach is less so, though on the face of it less efficient.

A user-driven approach is not planned or directed centrally. The contents of the knowledge base and the way it is used is decided by the users. I have seen user-driven knowledge bases spring up more or less spontaneously. More often they require a little push to get started. Where there is a central team, its role is to provide that push, make infrastructure and funding available, and support and facilitate what the users are doing. The key is to put the users in touch with each other. They can then decide how best they can help each other. They produce the material that goes into the knowledge base. If the material is not used, it dies and is replaced by new material. The users structure the material in a way that best serves their needs and, again, this structure morphs with usage. Large user groups divide themselves into smaller groups or communities of practice as they see fit. And these groups ensure that their members know the knowledge exists and how to find it.

There are certainly disadvantages to this approach: it can be slow (people have other priorities); it is messy; it is wasteful; and, sometimes, it never really gains enough momentum to get off the ground (although, arguably, this is because the need simply isn't there). But it does have two major advantages: participants get something that they actually use and which, consequently, brings value to the organization; and it tends to fit much better with the learning side of the knowledge equation than the centrally controlled approach.

Perhaps the obvious solution is to use the two approaches together. To some extent, you have to. But where you do this, you have to be careful that any central agenda does not interfere with or try to control the user initiatives. These rely on the good will of the participants and this can be lost very easily if they think that they are losing ownership.

Dealing with information overload and the 'runaway train' effect

Whichever approach you take to building your knowledge base, there is a risk that, once it is up and running, it can go out of control. I have seen this happen in two ways: information overload, where there is so much information in the knowledge base that it becomes extremely difficult to find anything you actually want to use and the whole process comes to a grinding halt; and a 'runaway train' effect where people get so involved in developing the knowledge base that it becomes an end in itself and distracts them from their main roles. While I readily accept that the second of these is less likely to happen with a consulting knowledge base than with more interesting subject matter, it often surprises me how easily people can get sucked in.

Information overload tends to be more of a problem with a centrally run knowledge base than with a user-driven one because users will tend to discard anything that they do not want to use, whereas with a central approach there tends to be more of an inclination to hold on to stuff 'just in case' and to introduce processes that *should* be beneficial rather than those that actually are.

Holding on to information is not necessarily a problem in itself. The problem occurs when this excess information obscures or obstructs the use of the information that people actually need and use. So it helps to make explicit the separation between knowledge that has a defined use (i.e. is an input to an active process that furthers your consulting objectives and features in defined use-cases) and that which does not. You should actively manage the former, checking its validity at regular intervals, updating it when additional information becomes available, ensuring it is easily accessible and clearly signposted. This might be the case, for instance, with information about the consulting teams that you regularly work with. The other information can simply be indexed and stored. In some cases you may even wish to organize it on several tracks with different levels of use and maintenance.

The overload issue can also be alleviated by providing synthesized or predigested knowledge to the users. By this I mean that someone goes through what your organization knows on a particular topic and pulls out the most useful material. Again, it is best if the users can be encouraged to do this themselves (because they are the best judges of what is useful), but they sometimes need a little prompting or some resource to help them. It is important to appreciate that this approach is only a partial solution because the most useful material for one situation is unlikely to be the most useful for another and some users will need to go deeper. So it is best to use this in parallel with the layering approach described above.

The problem of people allocating too much effort to the knowledge base can occur with either approach but for slightly different reasons: where the initiative is centrally driven, it generally happens because of misaligned incentives or unclear prioritization; where it is user-driven, it can occur because people perceive that they are gaining more influence and respect from their peers by contributing to and developing the knowledge base than by doing their normal jobs. Sometimes, whichever approach is taken, it is just a case of diminishing returns. It is rare in any activity for people to be able to spot the point at which a marginal effort ceases to yield a sufficient marginal return to be worthwhile.

The simplest solution to this issue is to prevent it from happening in the first place. For a central initiative, where you have more control, the standard toolkit includes your definition of scope and objectives, tracking, budgetary control and the alignment of incentives. For a user-driven initiative, although you have less direct control over them, there are some powerful checks and balances that come from the motivations that drive the participants: the desire to get better value out of consultants, to make specific projects succeed, to avoid failure and to be recognized by other participants, especially where they are organized in a group such as a community of practice. If someone gets carried away, they will cease to see the benefits as a user, and other users will not use their work.

Unfortunately, these mechanisms are not always effective. The control you have over a central initiative has to be exercised sparingly because, with knowledge management, there is really no way to know in advance how far you need to go to get the benefits and how far is too far. It is easy to misjudge this in either direction. User-driven initiatives usually fare better because they are, to some degree, self-regulating. But even for these there does seem to be a tipping point beyond which the knowledge stops serving its purpose and becomes an end in itself. The risk of this happening is, I would suggest, fairly high (which is why I have included this discussion in the book) and you need to be prepared for it.

How should you respond to this when it happens? The main thing is to avoid overreacting: It takes a lot or effort, skill and not a little luck to get a knowledge management 'machine' that really works and brings tangible value. It takes even more effort to consolidate and stabilise it. Before this consolidation and stabilization, it can be fragile and relies heavily on the good will and enthusiasm of the participants. So the last thing you want to do is disrupt this by running in like a bull in a china shop because of some perceived inefficiency in the way it is working.

The first thing to do is check that people are not, in fact, creating more value by contributing to the knowledge base than by whatever other activity they might be doing. Again, this is unlikely in the case of a consulting knowledge base, but do not assume so. Particularly with user-driven knowledge bases, there is often more value there than at first appears.

Secondly, try to understand how bad the problem actually is and whether it will sort itself out on its own: is it isolated or widespread? Is it recent or has it been going on for a while? The checks and balances that are built into both the central and the user-driven approaches—incentives in the case of the former and a kind of peer review for the latter—need time to work and it is quite normal to overshoot a bit before they kick in.

Thirdly, where you do need to intervene, look for indirect, long-term solutions. By finding mechanisms that will prevent the problem from recurring, you will be improving the overall knowledge management system rather than just fixing a problem. By using indirect measures (e.g. facilitating communications between the users and providers of information), you may be able to avoid some of the undesirable consequences of direct action.

Of course, there will be times when the only way to stop the train is through more robust and unambiguous measures. Just be aware that there will almost certainly be come collateral damage in the form of bruised egos, loss of motivation, good will and enthusiasm and, if you go too far, the collapse of any positive dynamic that had been established.

Creating a positive knowledge dynamic

This chapter has covered quite a bit of ground, so it is worth taking a step back to look at the key points:

- Knowledge is a key driver of the value you get from consultants
- It is important to take a broad view of knowledge—information is to knowledge what a car manual is to driving a car
- Consulting knowledge management can be implemented in different ways depending on how you currently work with consultants, your consulting objectives, your existing consulting knowledge and your organizational context
- An assessment of these factors will allow you to identify the role knowledge management should take in your consulting programme, focus that knowledge management

effort where it counts and make your approach work with, rather than against, your organization's strengths and culture

- Some form of consulting knowledge base, in which knowledge is captured and made available, is likely to be an important component of your knowledge management solution
- The knowledge base can take various forms and include different content, but to be effective it must be used. A small amount of knowledge with clearly defined use-cases is better than a lot of knowledge with none.
- Knowledge base projects can easily overshoot or go out of control. So it is important to build in some checks and balances and to remain watchful.

I have seen organizations assemble a knowledge base and leave it at that. Where it is well-implemented, this should bring some benefit. It should be apparent though, both from my initial emphasis on finding a balanced approach to knowledge management and from my frequent references to users and usage, that I think a knowledge-base-only approach is suboptimal. Once again, you increase the value you get from consultants by improving the decisions and behaviours that affect how you work with them. To achieve this, the knowledge that your knowledge base captures and makes accessible (along with other knowledge that may not be in the knowledge base) needs to be transferred into the heads of the people who are going to use it. In short, it has to be learnt.

I shall discuss it in detail in the next chapter, but before I do that, I would like to conclude this chapter by emphasizing the interdependence between your knowledge base and your learning processes.

The knowledge you capture in your knowledge base may come from many sources, but one of the main ones will be the lessons your organization has learnt from its (and its employees') experience of working with consultants. So learning is important for feeding your knowledge base. And this is not just passive learning, the lessons have to be extracted, analysed and synthesised before they can be collated and made available. If it is to work effectively, this process has to be managed.

Some of the knowledge that you capture in your knowledge base can be applied directly to consulting decisions. For instance, you may use your consultant database to identify an individual with a particular skill set. But much of the knowledge will need to be reviewed and assimilated before it can be applied. In other words, it will have to be learnt. The material you capture in your knowledge base is not just used for reference, but is also the basis for your organizational learning.

If you can get the right tension between the different elements, you should be able to create a self-sustaining, virtuous cycle: you work with consultants, you learn from this experience, you capture what you have learnt, you use this captured knowledge to learn how to do things better, you then apply what you have learnt and the cycle begins again. Knowledge that cannot be captured can still be included in this cycle, but has to be transferred directly.

Over time, this dynamic will lead to a steady increase in your organizational knowledge about consulting and, because this knowledge is applied, it will in turn become a capability and a source of value.

CHAPTER 6

Learning to Use Consultants

Knowledge management, the theme of the last chapter, is a relatively new management discipline. Organizational learning, on the other hand, has been around for a long time both as a field of academic study and as managerial practice, with contributions from many specialist areas. So I should begin this chapter by saying that I am not a specialist and make no claim to the kind of expertise that results from years of serious study and practice. What I do know, I have learned from implementing a range of learning programmes during the course of my consulting career and from a desire to keep myself informed on the subject. It is this knowledge, my experience of consulting and my knowledge of how consulting is used in a broad range of organizations that form the basis for this chapter.

Given these limitations, it would be fair to ask why I am trying to cover this subject at all when I could just refer you to the experts. There are three answers to this: firstly, although the field of organizational learning may be vast, there is next to nothing that covers learning how to work with consultants. So I hope my efforts here will at least provide a starting point and encourage the specialists to take a look at this area and correct or improve on my suggestions. Secondly, I feel that I need to emphasize learning: it is (almost by definition) critical to the development of any new capabilities and yet, in many organizations, it is almost an afterthought (although this situation does seem to be improving). And what is true for learning as a whole is doubly true of consulting because, where time and resources *are* given to learning, it tends to focus on things that are directly related to job performance rather than areas such consulting where the effects are indirect. Thirdly, assuming you do not already have a learning programme running, just getting the basic elements in place should bring significant benefits. So, by including these elements here, I am giving you all you really need to get started, which should save you a fair bit of legwork. Once you have implemented the basics, you can decide if you want to take things further.

Learning can be approached from many different directions (psychological, sociological, neurological, behavioural etc.). My focus here is mostly operational: getting the right structures, procedures and behaviours in place to ensure that the organization learns how to work with consultants. With this aim in mind, I split learning into two activities: the creation or discovery of new knowledge; and the transmission of knowledge (existing and newly acquired) into your organization so that more people are able to apply it. Both of these are called 'learning', but (except for some overlap) they are really quite different processes.

The structure of this chapter follows this split. It starts by looking at what you can do to promote learning from experience and the creation of new knowledge within your organization. (The possibility of acquiring knowledge externally does exist, but I do not intend to discuss it here). Then I shall cover transmission of knowledge. The third section highlights some characteristics of consulting as a topic for learning that may require particular attention. And the chapter concludes by looking at the role learning and knowledge management play in your broader consultant management programme.

Learning from experience

Before you can capture knowledge in your knowledge base, and before it can be shared in your organization, it has to be created, discovered or acquired. If you work with consultants frequently, there will already be a fair bit in existence when you start your consulting initiative and the purpose of creating a knowledge base is to capture or locate this. But there will come a point at which you will need to start generating new knowledge if you want to continue improving.

In most organizations, learning about consulting happens primarily in an *ad hoc* manner: an individual makes a mistake, realises it and adjusts his behaviour accordingly; or, conversely, they have a success, are rewarded and seek to repeat this experience. Most of this probably does not involve much conscious thought. Occasionally, someone might take the time to reflect on some work they have done with consultants, analyse it and draw some conclusions, but this is still likely to be an isolated exercise.

There are a couple of problems with this as a knowledge creation process: it is slow and inefficient; and it can often lead to the wrong lessons being learnt. The slowness and inefficiency are a result of the passive, haphazard nature of the process. Learning here is only a by-product. Little or no effort is made to learn and improve and not much time is spent analysing or reflecting on experience. The wrong lessons are learnt because people are drawing conclusions in isolation, with very limited or anecdotal data, no structure or rigour, and based on criteria that are largely random—they are based on the individual's mood at the time, on what their other preoccupations are, on their personal likes and dislikes, or even on what they had for lunch that day. As a result, valuable experience is wasted as a learning opportunity, or at least seriously underexploited.

The solution, in most cases, is not complicated: if ineffective learning is passive, haphazard and isolated, effective learning should be active, structured and collaborative.

Active learning

Active learning means that while you are working with consultants, you treat it as an opportunity to learn and you make the effort to exploit that opportunity. You do not have to devote a lot of time to active learning, but you do need to be consciously trying to learn from what you experience. You might, for instance, take a couple of minutes each day during a consulting project to ask what you have learnt and, just as importantly, what you think you could learn. The results will probably not be earth shattering, but the cumulative effect can be significant. The more people do it, the more significant the results will be and the more chance there is of someone having a eureka moment.

To achieve this, you need to cultivate a learning culture, where all those involved in working with consultants are trying to develop their expertise, whether they are on a project team or a steering group or (particularly) working in an area that is affected by the work consultants are doing. Learning should be looked upon as a skill to be developed in its own right.

You may already have a learning culture in place, backed up by sophisticated processes and infrastructure. But do you apply this to consulting? Even where a learning culture does exist, it does not often extend to 'non-core' areas like consulting.

If you do not have an established learning capability, you can try using the consultants to help you develop one. For them, learning is a core competence, both individually and collectively. Many introduce learning practices into the projects they work on and, by extension, to the client teams they work with. These teams should be encouraged to use the experience to learn about learning and you should not be embarrassed to ask the consultants to help. Most will be happy to do so and, once the project is complete, your project team members can share their newly acquired skills with others in your organization.

Structured learning

Having a culture of active learning is already a step change from passive learning, but there is still scope to make the learning more effective by introducing a degree of structure and organization into the learning process. Remember that we are still talking about discovering new knowledge here, so when I say structure and organization, you should not be thinking about schoolrooms, classes and syllabuses. This is more about ensuring that the thinking involved in generating new ideas and approaches gets done and that this effort is goal-driven and focused on the right areas. There is little point, for instance, in people spending a lot of time honing their consultant selection process, if they are not able to run basic steering group meetings effectively.

Organization, then, is about understanding your learning needs and planning how to exploit specific consulting experiences to meet these needs. Planning is the key—there is a world of difference between looking back at what has happened and asking 'what can we learn from this', and looking forward to ask 'what do we want to learn from this' before it has happened. In the latter case, you will be looking to answer specific questions that you have thought through beforehand and you will also have thought through how you are going to make your observations. You will effectively be treating your experience as a scientific experiment and should be in a much better position to draw conclusions from it.

This forward looking approach to learning can be taken even further by deliberately trying out different ways of doing things to discover what works best. Clearly, there can be some risks involved in this sort of 'test and learn' approach and it cannot be applied to all activities. It is particularly useful for low-risk processes that recur frequently (such as the steering group meetings mentioned above).

Some organizations go further than this and have standardized procedures for running these experiments. Although there are some disadvantages to this (it can be inflexible, for instance), it does reduce risk by providing thorough checklists, it can speed up the process considerably and it also creates a common language for people to discuss what they have learnt and how they learnt it. This makes the subsequent transmission of this knowledge much easier.

Organizing your learning also enables you to learn as a team (or even as an organization). There are many advantages to this that I shall discuss in the next section, but purely from an efficiency perspective, it means that the learning objectives can be divided up. This minimizes duplication (although some is necessary) and lets you cover more ground than when people are learning individually and trying to cover everything on their own.

By 'structuring' the learning, I mean putting in place groups, roles, objectives, processes, procedures, guidelines, templates, incentives, depositories and other structures that provide a framework in which learning happens. With this framework, people have a clearer understanding of what happens to the knowledge they create, where it might be used and applied and where new knowledge is needed. Where the framework includes targets and objectives (these should be used cautiously when it comes to learning) it can be used to set expectations. For instance, if people know that they are expected to write a 'thought piece' about a specific aspect of working with consultants at the end of the project they are currently engaged on, they tend to be far more productive than when they are simply tasked with learning as much as they can. Where objectives are not appropriate, incentives can take their place. You could introduce an element of competition by offering a title or a prize for the best ideas.

Both structuring and organizing the learning give you a certain amount of control over it. This is useful not only because it allows you to set the learning agenda, but also because it allows the learning to be monitored and the momentum maintained, if necessary by direct intervention. However willing the participants, when the pressure is high (as it almost always is during consulting projects) it is all too easy to leave learning for later or drop it altogether. With predefined and organized learning activities it is easier to prevent this or, at least, be aware when it is happening.

Collaborative learning

Maybe it is the idealist in me, but despite many examples to the contrary, I still cling to the belief that we are more productive and often more creative collectively than individually. When it comes to learning, I think the case for a collective effort is pretty compelling.

For a start, there is the efficiency gain I have already mentioned that comes from being able to share out the work. By learning together, you not only gain in efficiency, but also in effectiveness—you learn better. When several people look at the same events and discuss them, you remember far more and you see the situation from multiple angles. And when you discuss your interpretation of events with others who have shared the experience or who have other relevant experience, it forces you to be more rigorous in your own thinking and can provide validation for your conclusions. In short, when you learn collectively, you produce more knowledge, it is of better quality and more robust.

The involvement of more people can also help you organize the learning, because it permits a better understanding of your organization's needs and how they interrelate. And, of course, the more people are involved at the point of knowledge creation, the easier it is for that knowledge to be transmitted and distributed through your organization.

As with most good things, the benefits of collective learning come at a price. For once, though, it should not be a high one: it is mainly driven by the time spent communicating in order to share experience and discuss interpretations of it. The better organized and structured this is, the more productive it will be.

As most of this communication will be taking place between groups of people who share similar experiences, it should be reasonably easy, for the most part, to work out in advance what these groups will be: client teams who are working alongside consultants; teams and departments in your organization that are affected by the work consultants do; implementation teams that are tasked with implementing consulting recommendations; teams responsible for consulting relationships (if you have any); and, in many cases, the consultant teams themselves can also participate in your learning process. These groups already exist, so you do not have to expend any organizational effort in forming them. They simply need to be given the tools (procedures, templates, analytical support) and incentives that will make the collaboration easier and, importantly, that will set the expectation that it should take place.

Existing groupings within your organization will take you some way towards achieving your collaborative learning goals, but there will be issues for which these structures are more of a hindrance than a help. This is particularly true of consulting which tends to straddle traditional organizational boundaries. The best option for these situations are self-forming groups or networks, generally known as 'Communities of Practice'. These are networks of individuals who are involved in some aspect of working with consultants and have chosen to work together to improve their collective expertise at this particular practice. I shall not go into great detail about these networks here because they are central to much of the knowledge management literature, but I will just point out some of the key features:

- They are started by their members, so there is a motivational threshold that has to be crossed for them to be established (in other words, enough people have to want it badly enough).
- As the name suggests, they are communities of 'practice', not just of 'interest'. This means that areas of knowledge that they deal with are important to members' performance in their roles, or at least in some part of their roles. For our current purposes, this will be some aspect of working with consultants.
- They are knowledge-focused rather than task-focused
- Apart from creating new knowledge, they are the repository of knowledge on their chosen subject, communicate about this subject to the rest of the organization (and, at times, elsewhere) and are the first step in knowledge transmission.
- They are temporary because, at some point, there is no need to keep improving your knowledge in a given area. The members will generally sense that their own performance is not being improved sufficiently or that their knowledge is not in sufficient demand for it to be worthwhile continuing.

Although these networks effectively run themselves, there is quite a bit that you can do to encourage their formation. Awareness is key, to begin with: people need to understand what a community of practice is, what it involves and how to go about setting one up and running it. The best way to achieve this is to set one up (on any topic you choose, but preferably one that a lot of your organization can relate to), get it running and then let people know about it.

Once people are aware and a few of these communities are up and running, you need to provide them with the support they need. These needs will vary, but may include templates, facilitation, administrative support, collaboration tools, infrastructure and facilities (it seems to be getting harder and harder to get a meeting room in many organizations these days) and, in some cases, budget (although this is generally best left to the individual budget holders who are members of the community). The less time people have to spend organizing and administering their community, the more they will have to do what it was set up to do.

If these communities become part of common practice in your organization, it will be important to ensure that they function efficiently. You almost need a community of practice about communities of practice. At least, you need to establish what works and what doesn't, and develop a common language, structures and procedures that will allow greater speed and efficiency in setting up and operating them.

Transmitting knowledge

First hand learning of the kind I have described in the previous section is essential to generate new knowledge and to establish a core of people who are the custodians of this knowledge in your organization. Direct experience is also the only way that some forms of knowledge can be acquired. For instance, familiarity with a particular consulting firm can only really be acquired by working with them (however complete and forthcoming the firm's brochure may be). It is a good idea to identify these types of knowledge and the people who need it and to ensure that they get the exposure they need.

Not all knowledge has to be acquired by direct experience and this is just as well because otherwise your organization would quickly get bogged down reinventing ways of doing things that it already knows how to do. So the issue is how to transmit knowledge from the relatively few people who know it at the outset to the many people who need to use it if it is to be applied to the greatest advantage of your organization.

You have several things to manage here: the knowledge can range from complex (e.g. managing several consulting firms simultaneously on a major, technical project with a broad geographical remit) to fairly simple (steering group meeting); the audience for the knowledge can range from one person to many thousands (admittedly an extreme case), their learning requirements can be anywhere on the scale from superficial awareness to deep understanding and they will all have their own preferred learning styles; and the delivery can be intensive and personal (one-on-one coaching, shadowing and mentoring) or, at the other end of the scale, impersonal and directive (written procedures). You need to decide (or create a mechanism that decides) which knowledge to transmit to which people in which way.

I shall try to help you answer this question in what follows. You should bear in mind, though, that there are no easy recipes for knowledge transmission. Approaches that work well in some organizations do not work at all in others and what works on one criterion (e.g. absorption) may fail on others (speed, cost, reach...). It is a balancing act that requires some trial and error.

Who needs to know about consulting?

If your organization makes extensive use of consultants, then it is likely that most of your employees will need some understanding of how to work with them.

Buyers of consulting

The first group to look at are the managers responsible for commissioning consulting projects. Ideally, they should have

- Practical experience of operating a consulting project, preferably several
- Experience of defining requirements, negotiating and structuring consulting projects in terms of team selection, management and oversight
- A good knowledge of the consulting offerings in the market and of the alternatives available
- Familiarity with any consulting work that has been done in your organization, particularly where it is of a similar type to what they are thinking of commissioning
- A thorough grounding in your organization's own approach to using consultants
- Experience of working with the individual consultants in the past

There is quite a lot to learn here and it is not always practical for everyone who needs to bring in consultants to be on top of all of it. Far too often, though, not knowing is the default position and no effort is made to learn. Managers are expected to 'wing it', based on whatever past experience they may have and it is just assumed that, because of their seniority, they are quite capable of handling a consulting project. The more senior they are, the more it is assumed they know what they are doing.

While it is certainly true that having general experience at the senior levels of management helps, a lack of specific skills and knowledge about consulting is extremely risky for what is a critical role in any project. Given the stakes involved in some consulting work it should be a requirement that anyone commissioning such work has demonstrated a minimum level of competence. Maybe even a consulting 'driving test' would be a good idea.

Where the individual is unable, for whatever reason, to acquire a particular skill set, it is important that they are at least aware of what they are missing and where it is to be found in your organization.

Project managers

This is the other critical role in any consulting project. Sometimes it is the same person as the buyer, but not usually. They will need:

- Solid project management skills combined with experience of consulting projects
- Sufficient understanding of the methods the consultants employ to coach client team members
- A thorough knowledge of the client organization's policies and procedures concerning consultants
- An understanding of how your organization (and specific individuals within it) are likely to respond to the project
- A strong personal network in your organization that will enable them to get rapid access to people where needed, get information and 'oil the wheels' of the project
- An intimate knowledge of the proposal and contract agreed with the consultants (and any umbrella contracts)

and a good understanding of the implications this will have for the project

- Knowledge of how the project fits with other initiatives and activities and the ability to monitor these for anything that might affect the project
- A good understanding of the relationship between your organization and the consulting firm
- Ideally, some experience of working with the members of the proposed consulting team

It is not that common for all this knowledge to reside in one person. Where the project manager is aware of personal weaknesses and does not have time to acquire the knowledge, it is important that he or she include people with that knowledge in their team.

It is also worth looking at this knowledge as something that is never complete and that you can continue learning and developing over time as you build the competence to manage ever larger and more important projects.

Steering group members

Steering groups and project boards come in many shapes and sizes. They may include several roles: project director, interested parties, people who need to stay informed, people with specialist knowledge, sponsors, influencers and decision makers, to name a few. In view of this mix and the role that the steering group as a whole plays (to steer), the list of knowledge requirements is quite short:

- Context, rationale and objectives of the project
- How the project fits with other projects and activities
- What is actually happening in the project
- Specialist knowledge
- The role of the steering group and what it is not there for

- How to behave in meetings (ground rules and protocols)

As I said, it is a short list and should not be difficult to achieve. So it is a pity that so few steering groups do fulfil all these knowledge criteria, especially so because such failings can seriously undermine a project.

For steering groups, my advice is to keep it simple but to make sure that the simple things are done well. That means ensuring that everyone is properly briefed before and regularly during a project, that specialists contribute at the right time and in the right way (and, ideally, on their specialism) and that everyone understands how it is supposed to work, why it is there and what role they are supposed to play.

Project team members

These tend to be selected based on knowledge criteria:

- Their knowledge of and access to key resources
- Their networks (knowledge of people)
- Expertise in a specialist area

But they will have substantial learning needs as well. In fact, they often have the steepest learning curves of anyone involved in a consulting project. To begin with, they need to be familiar with:

- The background, objectives and scope of the project
- The political environment in which the project is run
- The methods that will be employed to do the work
- The consultants' working practices
- How to play the role of intermediary between the consultants and the organization
- How to communicate about the project

And they have to get up to speed on all this while keeping focused on the tasks in hand.

Implementation teams

For larger projects, it is not unusual to have an implementation team (with or without consultants) that is separate from the initial team. They need to know:

- How to communicate with the consultant team. This is a two-way communication—the implementation team needs to understand what they are being asked to implement and the consultants need to understand what the implications of their plans are likely to be
- The format of the consulting output
- Procedures and operating methods for working with the consultants, if this is what they are expected to do

As with the steering group, these are simple, practical knowledge requirements. They are nevertheless very important if the transition from planning to implementation is to be made successfully.

Support functions

The Finance, Human Resources and IT functions are very important information sources for consulting teams working in an organization. Generally, consultant information requests are managed on an *ad hoc* basis, with resource being allocated where it is available. Often one of the client team members is from one of the support functions and it is their role to liaise with their colleagues to get information that the project needs. This process can be very messy and lead to frustration on all sides, especially when the support functions are low on resources.

Some of the clients I have worked with have implemented measures to address this issue. These include standard information packages that they make available to consulting teams at the start of projects, data interfaces that allow project teams access to raw data, and operating procedures for interacting with these project teams that stipulate priorities and the level of service that they can expect to receive. These measures can be helpful, but they do not resolve the issue completely—by their nature, consulting projects tend to deal with non-standard data or with standard data in non-standard ways—but they do decrease the workload considerably and I would recommend them for any organization that makes frequent use of consultants.

Assuming you implement similar measures, your support functions will need to:

- Be familiar with the information packs, data sources and interfaces that are available
- Be able to advise users on how to use these
- Have specialists available with intimate knowledge of the data—there are always errors, anomalies and questions that can only be answered if you know how the data was collected and processed.
- Know the procedures for dealing with consulting teams and how to triage information requests
- Know the procedures for releasing confidential information
- Specific knowledge relating to their roles in certain types of consulting project (e.g. activity-based costing or process re-engineering) or for particular consultants

Areas affected by consulting projects and broader awareness

In discussing ways to increase the value of consulting to your organization, I introduced the idea of organizational receptiveness—a notional measure of how good your organization is at getting value from the consultants you employ. Receptiveness is not about being nice to consultants or, necessarily, about doing what they say. It is also about knowing how to question what consultants are doing and taking collective responsibility for ensuring that the outputs are as usable and useful to the organization as possible.

This is the greatest area of weakness (in their ability to work with consultants) in the organizations I have worked with. It is also, I suspect, the biggest area of opportunity for most organizations to get more value out of consultants.

To get at this value, you will need to work out what behaviours, attitudes, activities and procedures serve to increase receptiveness in your organization for the types of consulting projects you run and, critically, this knowledge must then be instilled in those employees who are going to be directly affected by consulting projects and, to some extent, in the broader workforce. It also means that employees (especially senior staff) who are not directly affected by a project should understand it sufficiently to be able to spot opportunities. These may be opportunities for them to contribute to the project or they may be ways in which the outputs of the project can also be turned to their benefit.

Consulting portfolio and relationship managers

These are roles that I shall introduce in the coming chapters. As the names imply, the consulting portfolio manager oversees your organization's portfolio of consulting projects and requirements to ensure balance, appropriate prioritization and co-ordination.

Relationship managers look after the relationship with individual consulting firms.

In most circumstances, the people in these roles will be net exporters of knowledge, but they also play a role as knowledge brokers and it is important that they be kept in the loop as new consulting knowledge is created so that they can pass it on to others in your organization.

External contractors and other consultants

You should not limit yourself to internal audiences for your knowledge transmission. By letting consultants know how you plan to interact with them, it allows them to prepare for this and, where necessary, adjust their own style and practices. It means that they can contribute to your organization's knowledge generation efforts by giving feedback on how they experience working with you and how your practices affect them. And it establishes a common platform for interaction on projects where multiple consulting firms are working alongside each other.

Transmission methods

All the groups discussed above have knowledge requirements, and different methods can be employed to transmit this knowledge. You will need to decide, for each audience, what the right blend of transmission methods is.

Crudely speaking, knowledge is transmitted by people who have knowledge communicating with people who need it. But this covers quite a range of different methods. At one end of the scale there is the direct exchange of knowledge. This may be as simple as a conversation or it may involve shadowing, supervision or coaching. Direct exchange is personal, one-to-one, time-intensive and capable of covering a topic in great depth, and is bidirectional, by which I mean that the learner can ask questions to validate and enhance their understanding. It is, I think, the only effective way of transmitting knowledge while it is still being created. At the other end of the scale you have documented procedures. These are indirect, impersonal, inflexible and one-directional, but they have the advantage of being able to deliver a simple message to many people in a resource-efficient way. Where the knowledge in question is simple and well-established, they bring a corresponding clarity and simplicity to the process. Somewhere in between the two, you have training. Depending on how this is done, it can be more towards one side of the scale or the other.

Managing knowledge transmission

The obvious answer is to use the method that is appropriate for the audience and for the type of knowledge being transmitted. So , for instance, you might introduce a set of procedures that lets your finance staff know how they should go about supporting a consulting project, but offer some more detailed training when one of them is seconded to a consulting project.

In principle at least, this is all reasonably straightforward: you review the knowledge that needs to be transmitted; you decide who needs it; and you package it for the appropriate transmission method.

In reality, though, three factors conspire to make things rather more complicated:

- *the instability of knowledge*—as knowledge is generated or collected, it is subjected to new inputs and multiple interpretations, discussions and experiments. This process is important because it validates the knowledge, completes it and makes it more robust. Until this process is fairly well advanced, however, it is difficult to gain the clarity needed for any formal transmission process to begin.

- *the difficulty of keeping track of knowledge as it is generated*—knowledge generation processes tend to be quite messy and unstructured.
- *the amount of knowledge*—learning programmes can quickly develop a life of their own and generate knowledge at a very fast pace. On the whole, this is a good thing. Clearly, though, controlling and managing this deluge, especially as it comes from many sources, is problematic.

So controlled or managed transmission (procedures, training and other structured exchanges) is only practical for the relatively small proportion of knowledge that has matured to the point where it is relatively stable.

This leaves a substantial proportion of the knowledge that is being generated and collected in your organization (by intent or otherwise) with no planned means of transmission. This is not as bad as it may sound—the fact that transmission has not been planned and organized does not mean that it does not happen. Whether or not you organize it and support it, people will still talk. Should you be doing anything about this or should you just let it run its course and wait until something is produced?

Yes and no. There is little point in trying to control this process—it would just suck up too much time and you would risk hobbling the very thing you want to encourage. But there are three things I think you should consider doing. The first is to provide encouragement, support and opportunity for these exchanges to take place (time, place and technology can all help). This may include introducing some measure of standardized process (such as review meetings and feedback forms) that help create a common language in which to transmit knowledge. They also have the side-benefit of allowing you to start capturing some of the knowledge earlier than you might otherwise have done. The second thing you should do is to try to keep an eye on what is going on. This may not always be easy to do, although it is made easier if you have entities such as communities of practice in place and they keep some record of what they are doing. Keeping tabs on the conversations that are happening will give you early warning of knowledge that is reaching a level of maturity where more formal transmission is appropriate and it also allows corrective measures to be taken when, as I have discussed in the previous chapter, people get carried away. And the third measure is to provide a path (preferably several) for people to formalize what they know and include it in your mainstream knowledge transmission.

You will need to assess how relevant these measures are for you and decide on this basis how much effort you need to put into each of them. You may decide that you should just leave people to their own devices and that any knowledge that is generated will eventually filter out. This is entirely legitimate, provided that you believe the learning culture in your organization is strong enough.

Best practice?

The avowed aim of many corporate learning programmes is to spread 'best practice' and I think this chapter would be incomplete without a brief discussion of it. I have designed and implemented such programmes on a number of occasions and have found best practice to be a very powerful concept, especially where it concerns relatively simple but pervasive processes and practices. So I would certainly recommend introducing some notion of best practice when it comes to working with consultants.

There are, however, a couple of limitations to best practice that you should take into account. Firstly, best practice is a consolidation mechanism and can prevent further improvement—by saying that something is already as good as it can be (or, more modestly, as good as you have been able to make it), you discourage people from looking for better alternatives. And however much you may argue that this is not how best practice is supposed to work, it is how it is often perceived in reality. You either need to accept this or develop a very strong culture to counter it. I am not sure this is worth the effort for consulting, but if you already have it, so much the better.

My second criticism of best practice is that, when it is applied to more complex processes or when it is based on too little experience, it can lead to a lack of flexibility. Where the effectiveness of a particular practice is sensitive to the particularities of the situation, the recommendations drawn from another (albeit similar) situation may not be appropriate. For instance, airtight contracts with consultants may be best practice in the US, but it can lead to unnecessary effort in many Asian countries where the written contract carries less weight. For these cases, you either need to create multiple versions of 'best practice' to cover all eventualities (not very practical), make it very clear in what circumstances it should be applied, or reduce its status from best practice to guidelines or examples of approaches that have worked in other situations.

Thirdly, I have noticed in some organizations that best practice can generate a bureaucracy of its own, with a best practice 'police' going around and ensuring it is followed. There may well be times when this is necessary, but in most cases that I have seen it has been counterproductive and should be avoided.

I would not want these issues to prevent you from introducing the concept of best practice in your work with consultants. It is, as I have said, a powerful tool. Just be cautious about where you use it.

Consulting-specific considerations for your learning programme

The discussion in the last two sections has been largely generic— learning about consulting mostly involves the same principles as learning about anything else. In this section, I will focus on the peculiarities of consulting that may lead you to deviate from these general principles or to adjust the emphasis of your learning programme.

Lack of continuity and repetition

Most organizations (and, even more so, the individual employees within them) experience consulting as a temporary, punctual event: requirements are defined; consultants come in; you work with them; they leave. An individual employee is unlikely to work with the same set of consultants or on the same type of project more than once. This can make it difficult for that individual to draw out the lessons from their experience. This underlines the importance of organizing your learning programme so that lessons are learnt and conclusions are drawn based on collective experience.

This lack of repetition in the individual experience of consulting also makes it difficult to acquire any skills that require practice because you simply do not engage in the activity often enough. For instance, you could compare the facility you develop with a sales or training presentation that has been given many times and honed in the process to the (generally) much more tentative process of organizing knowledge transfer at the end of a consulting project.

This issue is not as problematic as it may at first appear. The notion that no two consulting projects are the same is only partly true and you can close some of the experience gap by breaking down the work you do with consultants into its component parts (the consulting process described in Chapter 3 should provide a starting point). Although the projects may be different, many of these parts will be similar. Where a particular skill set is considered important, the objective should be to expose the individual to as many instances of that particular activity as possible. This may involve bringing them in as process specialists or observers for that stage of projects that they may not otherwise be involved in. They could even be seconded on projects outside your organization, with partners, suppliers or customers. The advantage of this kind of exposure is that they are likely to be under less pressure than they would be if they were responsible for delivering the project, there are no conflicting objectives and they can focus on learning. This approach of giving individuals maximum exposure to a focused area of activity is one that I have used quite a bit in my consulting and have found it to be very effective. So I would recommend that you consider it where you feel that you have a skills gap that needs filling.

When the opportunities for direct exposure to an activity are limited, it may be possible to supplement this with training and rehearsal. This provides a safe environment for exploring options and practising skills and techniques. It is not ideal, though, because it usually requires an expert to set it up and run it and, however accurate the simulation, it never feels quite like the real thing.

High-pressure environment

Live consulting projects are usually high pressure environments. Although it is important for people to be exposed to this as part of their learning, it can also hamper that learning: when people sense that they are under pressure to deliver and to do so on a very short timescale, they develop a kind of tunnel vision, focusing exclusively on the task in hand and are unwilling or unable to take a step back and look at how they are doing it, or whether they could do it differently or better. Often this is compounded by the fact that, for the individual in question, the consulting project is a new environment with new people and new ways of doing things, and they have to work out how to deal with all this before they can actually start performing effectively. Then, typically, when the project ends, they move on to other things and do not take the time to assess what they have done.

This scenario, of course, holds true in many areas of activity, but I think it is almost systematically the case for consulting projects. While I understand why people respond this way and, having been in this position, have some sympathy for them, the outcome is that a learning opportunity is lost.

To learn how to deal with this, it is worth taking a look at the approach employed in sport. The problem of learning while under pressure is encountered in many sports, especially at the elite level where it is no longer possible to rely on physical conditioning and raw talent alone and there is a constant pressure to improve. In sport, the pressure is physical as well as mental and emotional, and participants are often performing at the limit of their abilities. But they still have to find ways to learn and improve. So they develop a state of self-awareness in which they are able to observe themselves, monitor their performance and identify weaknesses as they arise. A similar awareness can be developed in the organizational context and, fortunately, it is much easier to do because the pressures are not as high and the need for sensitivity is not as great. Developing these skills, learning about learning, takes a little effort, but the skills can then be applied in many areas.

Noise

Another factor that can impede learning is the 'noise' and confusion caused by all the communications around consulting projects. These come from multiple sources and can take many different forms: the project will usually have its own communications that are intended to further its objectives; the consultants will want to promote themselves by highlighting their role in any successes (and downplaying failures and errors); interested internal parties will also have their axes to grind in pursuit of their different agendas. It is a politicised environment, messages get mixed, waters get muddied and it can be difficult to interpret experience and draw lessons from it.

There is, as far as I can see, nothing that can be done to change this. It is simply a reality that you have to be aware of and take into account as best you can.

Attitudes

Lastly, as with knowledge management, attitudes to consultants will be a key influence on how you learn to work with them. The point I would like to make here is that the effect attitudes have is not always straightforward. It is not simply the case that organizations which have negative attitudes learn less and those with more positive attitudes learn more. For a start, it is not really possible to talk about an organization's attitude to consultants—most organizations harbour a range of individual attitudes, from consulting 'groupies' to the outright hostile, and it is unwise to assume these will just average out. Negative attitudes can actually be good for learning because people who distrust consultants often feel the need to be better prepared to deal with them.

Similarly, people who are very positive about consultants (they do exist) may not be as critical as they need to be if they are to learn and improve.

Consultant responses

As you learn about consultants and adapt your organization's behaviours based on this learning, consultants will adapt their behaviours too because they are constantly trying to find ways to improve their position with your organization. This can be confusing because, just when you think you have found the best way of doing something, it turns out you have not—the goal posts are moving constantly. Sometimes these changes in consultant behaviour may be to your benefit and sometimes they may not.

You need to ensure that your learning keeps pace with these changes so that you can adapt at least as fast as the consultants. But, rather than getting locked into a perpetual arms race, it is worth thinking about how consultants will react before you try to introduce changes in your own behaviour. If you do this, you should be able to steer these changes in consultant behaviour and align them more closely with your interests.

By way of conclusion to this section on the consulting-specific aspects of learning, I should emphasize that the points I have included here are nuances that should help you steer your learning programme and get the best out of it. But they are only really relevant once you have worked out the fundamentals of your consulting learning programme.

Learn first

The normal approach to getting more value out of consultants would probably start with careful analysis, be followed by a redesign of processes and procedures, and culminate in planning and implementation. Maybe afterwards you might think about bringing in some training to consolidate the new processes and ensure that the changes stick. This is very much the way I thought about it when I first approached the issue.

As I looked into it further, though, it became clear to me that this approach had limitations and that a more knowledge-led approach was needed. I became convinced that, while there is value in efficiency improvements (which is what an analytical approach primarily targets), there is probably far more to be gained from improving organizational receptiveness. A lack of receptiveness can be put down (mostly) to people's knowledge, mental models and attitudes—attitudes that result in part from fragmented and incomplete knowledge. So to improve receptiveness, you need to foster a learning culture.

There are other reasons, too, why I think knowledge management and learning are a good starting point. Firstly, it is relatively easy to do—a few simple review procedures in the right place and a bit of knowledge mapping are enough to start generating value. For those of us who have struggled implementing overly-complex 'solutions' this reason alone is probably enough to convince. And, as you will have noticed, most of the knowledge that will help you get more out of consultants is not terribly sophisticated. It is more about having the capability to do simple things consistently and well. This is why knowledge transmission is so important. Secondly, as I point out in the last chapter, there is probably quite a bit of knowledge already in your organization. You just have to harness it. Thirdly, even if it turns out not to help with consulting (although I am pretty sure it will), developing your learning and knowledge management capabilities is beneficial in itself, so this is a very low risk approach.

The final reason is that you probably do not know how far you can take this and how much value there is in it. Nor do I think you can work this out analytically without putting in a lot of unnecessary effort. When you are setting objectives in a well established area, there is a wealth of comparative and historical information available that allows you to assess what is achievable. This is not the case for consulting. Any objectives you set for this area will either be limited to what you know already, require a lot of analytical work or be aspirational rather than realistic. If you can establish a low-risk heuristic (learning) process that is constantly running in the background as you work with consultants, you will spare yourself much of the analytical work and, over time, develop a much clearer picture of where the value lies.

I do not want to discourage you from doing your homework, understanding the value drivers and setting objectives. On the contrary, I think the lack of rigorous thinking in this area needs to be addressed if you are to develop a more professional approach to working with consultants. But I have also seen how powerful a learning-based approach can be. Given that it should also be low-risk and low-cost, I do not think you should wait until you have completed your analysis before you start the learning. It does not have to be on a grand scale or in any way comprehensive. Just get the ball rolling early and, by the time you have done your analysis and worked out your objectives, you should have a process running that is providing you with information and insights and is already generating value.

CHAPTER 7

Your Consulting Portfolio

In the last two chapters, we looked at how building a consulting knowledge base and developing the organization's competencies in working with consultants can help to establish an environment in which you drive more value from the consulting projects you undertake and the consulting relationships you maintain. But, however good you may be at the individual aspects of working with consultants, there is scope to enhance this further by balancing and co-ordinating consulting activities across your organization.

In Chapter 4 we looked at how this lack of co-ordination causes value to be lost: duplicated work, increased overheads, unnecessary projects (or projects that are inappropriately staffed) and a loss of alignment between functions and business units. If you add up all the instances of this kind of value leakage, it is often substantial.

Stemming the value leakage is the first level in getting more value out of consulting and it focuses primarily on cost and efficiency. The second level is to look at each piece of consulting work that you commission as an investment with a cost, an expected return and an associated risk, and to find ways of maximising the return while minimizing the cost and risk. (This may sound obvious, but it is surprising how rarely it is done). The third level involves looking at all the consulting work you do collectively, as a portfolio. Co-ordination of this portfolio can open up opportunities to leverage and combine benefits, to share or avoid costs, and to offset or mitigate risks. As with an investment portfolio , you can manage the profile of your consulting portfolio and each new consulting project you commission will affect this profile and changes the balance of your overall portfolio.

Most of the time, the decision to invest in a consulting project will take place in an environment where capital is constrained and so for every project that is authorized, an opportunity cost is incurred. Where this is not taken into account, capital is allocated suboptimally and value is lost.

Before everyone runs off to build their portfolio optimization models, I should point out that very few organizations succeed in co-ordinating their consulting activities at the most basic operational level and I have seen none that have managed it at the portfolio level. This is not altogether surprising: in most organizations, the co-ordinating role simply does not exist and implementing a co-ordinated approach to managing your consulting portfolio (let alone optimizing it) involves overcoming several serious obstacles.

To begin with, the client organization is often not that well co-ordinated itself, especially when it has many different units performing different activities or when it has a broad geographic spread. Even when these obstacles are not present, office politics, interdepartmental rivalries, budgetary autonomy and poor communications structures all make the task of co-ordination more difficult.

This situation is often not helped by the consultants themselves: in their eagerness to get the sale, consultants sometimes play one part of an organization off against another. They are also not famous for working well with their competitors—usually one firm pushes the others to the sidelines. I would like to be able to say that it is usually the best firm that comes out on top in this scenario, but in reality success more often comes down to political influence, manipulation and horse-trading.

From a management perspective, your consulting portfolio is actually three portfolios in one: the portfolio of requirements or needs within your organization which could be addressed by using consultants but which have not yet formed into projects; the portfolio of consulting firms and individuals with which the organization has a relationship; and the portfolio of past, current and proposed projects. These components are highly interdependent and any initiative to co-ordinate one of them is likely to fail if the others are not managed at the same time.

On top of this, the value that can be achieved from the consulting portfolio does not depend solely on the performance of the individual investments but is dependent on a constantly changing organizational environment. A project that starts out promising enormous benefits to the organization can easily turn out to produce no value at all, not because it is ill-conceived or badly run, but because the organization has moved on and its needs have changed.

Lastly, before we push the portfolio analogy too far, we should bear in mind that consulting projects are not tradeable assets: they (usually) have no resale value. This increases the risk profile substantially, although this risk is mitigated to some extent by the level of control you have over the performance of individual 'investments'. But in order to mitigate the risk, you have to be able to exercise the control, which brings us back to the need for co-ordination.

So a consulting portfolio is messy, constantly changing, subject to high levels of uncertainty and multiple outside influences. As such, it does not lend itself readily to the optimization techniques and quantitative tools that might be applied to a simpler portfolio of discrete, liquid investments with quantifiable, diversifiable risks. But this does not mean that we should just throw up our hands and give up. While I agree that you are unlikely to ever get a fully optimized, balanced consulting portfolio (if that even means anything in this context), there are plenty of things to be done to improve the situation and sometimes this improvement can be dramatic. In this chapter I shall explore some of the practical measures you can take to get a grip on your consulting portfolio and overcome the obstacles I have described above.

A path to portfolio management

Given that most organizations are likely to be starting from scratch in managing their consulting portfolio and given also that it is likely to be a fairly long journey, I would suggest dividing it up into a series of steps. I use five—rationalization, monitoring and support, consulting strategy, co-ordination and partnering—which I describe below in terms of objectives, key activities, obstacles to be overcome and capabilities to be developed.

The main rationale behind having these five steps is to avoid biting off more than you can chew and to allow you to build up and consolidate your capabilities as you go. I suggest you adapt the steps (or create your own) to suit your own context and requirements.

Rationalization

If you are a heavy user of consulting, sorting through and cleaning up your existing portfolio is likely to be no small task.

- *Objectives*—primarily to eliminate waste, but also to build the foundations for the portfolio development that is to come.
- *Key activities*—information gathering, collation and analysis (part of building your knowledge base); investigating, reconfiguring, consolidating and shutting down projects (but bearing in mind the caveat about tinkering with live projects); reallocating resources.
- *Obstacles*—the key obstacle is likely to be opposition and a lack of cooperation, not just from the consultants, but from people in the organization who have invested time, money and reputation in particular projects or who consider themselves (maybe rightly) to be better judges of the value of the project than someone who has not been involved.
- *Capabilities*—a better knowledge of how your organization is using consultants and greater awareness of this across the organization; a clearer understanding of the consulting firms you are engaged with; experience of assessing and restructuring consulting projects that can be used as an input to specifying future projects; some understanding of how consulting activities in your organization link to each other.

Monitoring and support

Once you have sorted out your existing portfolio, you need to look to the future and begin to manage consulting requirements before they become projects. In some organizations it may be possible to simply set up a central function that controls all the consulting contracts. Although I agree that there is some kind of central role here (real or virtual), I see it more as a support role or centre of excellence at this stage. You risk rejection if it is viewed as some sort of 'consulting police'.

- *Objectives*—to monitor and assess consulting activities in your organization on a continuous basis; to understand current and future consulting requirements; to provide buyers of consulting with support based on this information; to earn the trust of the buyers in the support role and to develop their understanding of how it can bring value.

- *Key activities*—defining and setting up the central roles; project monitoring; needs assessment; knowledge base development; developing an advice and support service for buyers of consulting.

- *Obstacles*—resourcing the central roles; perception of new roles as control rather than support.

- *Capabilities*—a clearer understanding of the resource mix in your organization (internal vs. external), how this mix can be flexed and to what effect; skills in scoping and refining consulting requirements; increasing awareness on the part of buyers and other staff of the role consulting plays and the advantages of managing the portfolio.

Consulting strategy

It is at this stage that you actually begin introducing some elements of central co-ordination, with managers looking at the bigger picture beyond their own, immediate consulting requirements. The advice and guidelines that have been offered as part of the support function can be brought together in a consulting policy or strategy. This phase should only begin once the support role is well established and has been sufficiently successful for managers (buyers of consulting) to be convinced that there is value in having common consulting goals and a strategy for achieving them.

- *Objectives*—establish a track record; buy in for a co-ordinated approach; extend the time horizon for needs assessment; draft a strategy; communication of strategy.
- *Key activities*—continue advisory/support role; track value from co-ordination; start integrating with broader resourcing strategy; begin sharing approach with key consultants.
- *Obstacles*—complexity, resources (there is quite a lot of work here).
- *Capabilities*—understanding of which aspects of portfolio management can benefit your organization; alignment around the strategy; portfolio considerations are now part of the commissioning process; deep, context-specific understanding of how to apply consulting resources.

Co-ordination

By this stage, the role of the portfolio manager (or team) is established. They are seen as experts and are involved in all consulting-related activities. Consulting requirements are anticipated and assessed in the context of your broader requirements, risks, available funds and existing consulting activities. Alternatives to new projects (such as extensions of old ones) are actively sought. These anticipated requirements now represent the largest part of the consulting work you commission and separate arrangements are in place for *ad hoc* work. All staff who are involved or affected by consulting projects have some understanding of the consulting strategy. Your key consulting partners are kept informed of future requirements on a regular basis.

- *Objectives*—to have an actively managed, balanced consulting portfolio; establish a dialogue and joint planning with key partners
- *Key activities*—broader communication of consulting strategy; set up processes for implementing strategy; put in place systematic communications with partners; continue monitoring needs and activities.
- *Obstacles*—broader audience to convince; willingness of consulting partners to share information.
- *Capabilities*—medium term planning of consulting; relationship management; broader application of skills developed in earlier phases.

Partnering

If you have completed the previous stage, you will already be effectively managing your consulting portfolio. In the partnering phase, your consulting portfolio becomes fully integrated with your management of consulting relationships. Resource and requirements planning is now a joint exercise with your consulting partners and systematically takes into account their plans and resource availability.

- *Objectives*—to achieve a much tighter integration with your chosen consulting firms so that you jointly manage your consulting portfolio
- *Key activities*—joint needs assessment, requirements development and resource planning; put in place umbrella contracts to enable quick deployment of key suppliers
- *Obstacles*—trust (or lack of it); management overhead; risks of partnering with the wrong suppliers
- *Capabilities*—integration and working together with external parties at all levels of the organization.

I appreciate that real life is unlikely to follow such a neat series of steps and I have seen organizations that have already implemented elements of the fourth and fifth steps without really having dealt with the first. There is nothing intrinsically wrong with this and I have seen it work out well. In other cases, it has not worked so well because the foundations (structures, capabilities, mindsets, relationships) were not there to support the more complex tasks being undertaken. So this is worth paying attention to, whichever sequence you opt for in implementing portfolio management.

Negotiating the obstacle course

It will be apparent from the previous sections (and from Chapter 4) that building a portfolio management capability is something of an obstacle course and the whole process will run far more smoothly if you have made preparations to deal with these obstacles in advance. The first step is to be realistic in your expectations. If you have a large organization which is spread across 50 countries and has 10 different and largely independent activities, you should not expect (and may not need) to achieve global co-ordination of consulting, at least not overnight. For instance, it probably makes sense to develop better co-ordination at the local or functional level before you try to build it at a global level. And it is a good idea to focus efforts on areas where you feel that you can achieve results quickly. This will build confidence in the process and make subsequent actions easier to implement. This is particularly true during the rationalization phase in which you will have to pick your battles wisely if you are to avoid getting bogged down in political in-fighting and personal agendas that may have little or nothing to do with what you are trying to achieve.

Getting the budget holders on-side

Once you have worked out this phasing and before you launch the project in earnest, you need to create an environment in which it can succeed—a critical element of this is getting the budget holders on board. And it isn't enough to get them paying lip service to a set of general goals—you need to build sufficient consensus, commitment and motivation for this to be reflected in their behaviour.

How you get them on board depends on the individuals involved, on the structure of the organization and on the way consultants are currently used. In some cases the rational argument will suffice. In others, you will have to use key influencers, peer pressure, status and other political and emotional levers to bring them around to the view that a co-ordinated approach is not only in their own best interests, but sufficiently beneficial to warrant them putting some effort in (and making some sacrifices) to achieve.

Facilitation and communication

With all the key people aligned, you should not leave them hanging around, waiting for something to happen. Even if they are genuinely committed to the objective, they have other responsibilities which take precedence and are unlikely to drive it on their own. Despite this, co-ordination will not happen without them because they are the ones commissioning and running the projects. So they will need structure, support and guidance to help them co-ordinate their activities with those of others. If they are convinced of the value the consulting initiative can bring, they will probably also want to be kept informed about and involved in it so that they see the progress and the benefits being delivered. This is a major part of the portfolio team's role. The better they are at it, the more people will see the benefits and the more the project will gain momentum.

Consultants and politics

The next obstacle to tackle is the consultants. Specifically, you need to stop them manipulating the politics of the organization to win individual projects. Your aim should be to align their success more closely with the overall, long-term welfare of the organization. Although the client organization has considerable power here, this influence is dissipated when it comes down to individual buyers—many consulting sales teams will follow a 'divide and rule' approach, setting one manager or one department against another. What is more, many managers will play along with this, seeing the consultants as their allies in dealing with organizational politics.

One response to this is to present a united front, with no single manager responsible for buying decisions. Although this approach is good in theory, it remains quite easy to manipulate unless very strong discipline is maintained. This is especially true in situations where the decision panel do not agree with each other: the consulting firm that has the strongest relationship with the highest-ranking manager tends to win. The other effect of the 'united front' approach is that the interaction with the consultants becomes much more formal. In some cases this can be a good thing. But in many consulting projects it is important to build a strong and fairly intimate relationship between the main protagonists and this tends to be undermined if the initial interactions are too formal and impersonal.

Another way to prevent manipulation (and the one I prefer) is to render it unnecessary by sharing your portfolio thinking and your nascent requirements with senior consultants and relationship managers. If the consultants know that, to win work, they need to make their proposals fit the portfolio rather than just the specific requirements for the project (and you can explicitly make future contracts dependent on good behaviour), they will shift their focus away from the personal interests and preferences of the individual buyer and try to influence the portfolio. True, they will still be trying to promote their own interests, but, at this level, they will have to do so by presenting a case rather than by being divisive and setting people against each other. And, as an added benefit, you get free advice on the structure of your portfolio.

Managing competition between consultants

Dealing with rivalries between consulting firms is a balancing act, because some level of competition is desirable. If you try to design your portfolio of consulting suppliers so as to avoid all areas of overlap, you leave yourself exposed if your chosen supplier is unable (for whatever reason) to help you on a particular project and you have to resort to another firm which you do not know so well, with which you do not have a relationship or which is not as well qualified for that particular task. Where you have only one preferred supplier for a given area, it puts you in a relatively weak negotiating position and you do not get the benefit of two or more firms thinking about the problem.

Ideally, the aim is to create an environment where consultants compete on merit and where they are willing and able to work together when this suits your needs. If you managed to realign the consultants to focus on the portfolio rather than the project, then you are well on your way to achieving the first of these. The second is relatively easy to achieve if the consultancies in question can be confident of a decent amount of work from your organization—the bigger the pie, the more to go around. Where this is not the case, it is up to you (the portfolio team) to make the suppliers understand that either they work together in your interests or not at all. You can also point out that you are looking at their ability to co-operate with each other as a measure of how well they co-operate with you. This should achieve the desired result, provided the portfolio manager has the necessary seniority, skills and, above all, a strong enough mandate, supported by other managers in the organization.

Tracking your portfolio

The last piece of the portfolio management jigsaw is information. I have raised the subject before in Chapter 4, but it bears repeating in this context. Without accurate, timely information about consulting activities in your organization, the level of co-ordination that can be achieved is fairly limited: as the consulting portfolio is bought by many different people, the only way that the organization can present a co-ordinated buying approach is if there is good information available to all those involved. The implication of this is that some form of project and relationship tracking system needs to be in place if you are to make portfolio decisions. If this is linked to the database of consultants described earlier, it can be a powerful tool.

The ease or difficulty of putting such a tool in place depends on what is already there, how well integrated your systems are, the quality of communications and information sharing within the organization and geographical dispersion. In an organization which has multiple international units that operate independently using their own IT systems and which does not have any project tracking in place, the cost of setting this up might well outweigh the benefits (and there are probably other issues to be addressed before looking at portfolio managing consulting projects). On the other hand, putting in place some sort of project tracking across the organization has benefits well beyond the management of consultants and a rudimentary system or process need not be very costly. Just maintaining a list of all the projects currently running is a good start.

More sophisticated systems track the progress of projects from initial requirements through to post-completion review. They also cover the resources and suppliers used by each project, predict resource requirements and show dependencies between projects (both in terms of resources and deliverables).

Clearly this sort of tool is great for balancing resources across multiple projects, but it can also be used analytically to help your organization benchmark and improve its overall project and portfolio management capability.

Building portfolio management capability

Portfolio management of consulting can deliver benefits faster than the other elements of the consulting mix. This is largely because, in most organizations, you are likely to be starting from a relatively low base and the first stage of portfolio management is to rationalize your existing projects.

After the early wins, however, subsequent benefits take a little longer to achieve because quite a lot has to happen: the portfolio team must establish and consolidate its role; budget holders have to be brought on board; and a certain amount of organizational inertia has to be overcome. All of this takes time for your organization to assimilate.

Perhaps the most tricky aspect of adopting a more co-ordinated approach to consulting (and the one that requires the most time) is that you have to learn how to do it as you go. As I mentioned at the start of the chapter, it is a fairly new idea, at least in this context. There are no guidebooks or business school case studies. You are unlikely to have done it before and you are equally unlikely to know anyone who has. So you have to apply insights gained from experience elsewhere. You have to be willing to try things out. And your learning radar has to be turned on and tuned in to pick up what works and what doesn't. All this, of course, can be greatly facilitated if you have a consulting knowledge base and learning disciplines already in place beforehand.

I am convinced that the benefits of co-ordination increase as portfolio management is extended from support to co-ordination and, potentially, further to the more strategic role of defining and overseeing the organization's consulting policy and objectives. But to achieve your potential in portfolio management, you have to focus some effort into developing and managing your relationships with consultants. This is the subject of the next chapter.

CHAPTER 8

Relationship Management

Relationship management is the final component of your consultant management toolkit. Like the others, it brings substantial benefits in its own right, but has limitations if it is not used in combination. So, before going into it in more detail, it is worth casting our eyes back over the previous chapters to see how it fits in: developing a knowledge base makes better-informed decisions possible, but does not ensure that the competencies are in place to make them. The competency issue can be addressed through learning, both in terms of knowledge generation and transmission, but this still leaves you with the problem of co-ordinating multiple consulting projects, potentially across multiple geographies, functions, entities and timescales. So we introduce an element of co-ordination and try to look at the projects as a portfolio. This too has its limitations because of the way consulting projects are commissioned and run and because of the techniques that consultants use to sell them. Relationship management helps to address these issues and, if well implemented, can also change the way consultants bring value to your organization: if the consultants feel that there is more value in the long-term relationship than there is in a specific project, they will think twice about pushing for a sale at any cost. As a result, their interests become much more closely aligned with yours, their focus changes and they start thinking not only of how they can solve the problem you have given them, but how to benefit your organization in the long run.

Why develop consulting relationships?

The benefits of building a relationship go well beyond alignment—it reinforces each of the other components of the consulting mix. By developing a strong relationship, you can get more information about the consulting firm and are in a position to ask for it directly, without having to piece together bits and pieces gleaned from multiple sources. Conversely, the consulting firm can build up a much more complete and detailed picture of your organization. The more complete this picture and the more people in the consulting firm who are familiar with it, the more efficient and effective the consulting work is likely to be. The consultants will also spend much more time thinking about your organization, even when they are not engaged on a project. Given the opportunity, most will be happy to share these thoughts, especially if they feel their ideas will be listened to. They treat this as the exploratory phase of their sales process, but for the client, this is not only a source of insights, but can be a very useful sounding board for management's own ideas.

As I mentioned earlier, consultants do not only do projects. Building the relationship provides an opportunity to explore the formats for such interactions, to participate in other activities alongside consultants and to tap into the (often substantial) information and research resources which consultants have at their disposal.

For instance, consultants can be used on an advisory basis to participate in board discussions, think tanks or project steering groups. Consultants regularly carry out research as part of their service development or to build their understanding of a particular industry or management issue. Participating in this kind of research alongside the consulting firm can yield valuable insights and information. Consultants also run or moderate discussion groups, networks and benchmarking groups. A good working relationship helps you make the most of these opportunities and allows you to influence them more directly. On a more mundane level, consultants can often provide quick answers to those questions which crop up from time to time and which might otherwise require some time and effort to resolve.

These are just a few examples. As your organization builds its relationship with a consulting firm, more possibilities will become apparent. Some of these may be small, but when they are taken together and if they are exploited properly, they can transform the cost/benefit equation of using consultants.

Becoming more competent at using consultants will improve the overall relationship—consultants generally prefer to work for people who know what they are doing. Conversely, a good relationship will enhance this competence by enabling a much freer flow of information and feedback to and from the consultants.

Lastly, a strong relationship, if well managed, can greatly improve the co-ordination of consulting activities within the organization by making consultants part of the portfolio management process. Such early involvement costs the organization nothing, can greatly accelerate project set-up (because consultants can align their resources for future projects), and makes for better planning of projects (because the consultants have seen how requirements have evolved and participated in this evolution).

Assessing your relationships

The illustrations above should give some idea of the benefits and opportunities that a strong relationship can bring. But what is a 'strong' relationship in this context? To answer this, it is perhaps easiest to start by looking at what it is not.

I have often heard consultants saying that they have a strong relationship with a client organization when, in fact, all that exists is a personal relationship between a senior consultant and the organization's CEO. One also hears of 'strong' relationships where there are friendships between individuals in the client organization and the consulting firm. Others try to express the strength of the relationship in numbers—how many people from the organization know how many from the consulting firm or how many projects have been completed. And others talk about how well they have worked together and may point to specific instances of successful collaboration.

These elements can help a relationship along, but they are no guarantee that the relationship is a good one: a one-on-one relationship between senior executives does not mean that the two organizations have a relationship—what happens when one of the individuals leaves? And personal relationships can also be divisive, especially when that relationship is seen to be the reason for choosing one consultant over another.

Social relationships are not the same as relationships between organizations, which must be measured in concrete benefits and not in the number of dinner parties attended or rounds of golf played. Organizational relationships should not be confused with 'friendships'. The individuals involved do not even have to like each other (although this can help), but they do, collectively, have to enhance each other's productivity. And where there are multiple relationships between individual employees, they remain fragmented unless they are co-ordinated and channelled into a group effort.

People often think that if organizations work together enough, a relationship will develop. It will, but it is likely to be disorganized, fragmented, patchy and difficult to control. It is also difficult to make this kind of organically developed relationship economically productive if a layer of structure is not introduced.

The key to making a consulting relationship work is to understand that it is a relationship between organizations—and a commercial one at that. As such, it is successful only if it creates value for both parties and, crucially, that this value is shared in a way that both parties perceive to be fair. Highly successful relationships fall apart because one side perceives the other to be taking more than its fair share of the benefits.

The relationship-building process

The starting point in building your relationships is thus to develop a common understanding of what both parties stand to gain. Attempts at relationship management are often left at this, with the assumption that a rough outline of potential benefits is enough to make the relationship run smoothly. It certainly helps, but I firmly believe that consulting relationships yield far more value if they are designed, monitored and actively managed. The key steps in doing this are: defining objectives, creating the role of relationship manager, relationship design, initiation of key activities, and assessment of results.

Relationship objectives

Over the course of this book, I have looked at some of the ways the client can derive value from consulting relationships. For the consultant, the most obvious benefit of moving away from a transactional approach is more (and more efficient) sales to the client organization. Given the costs of selling consulting, almost any process which could reduce these costs merits serious consideration and there are other things that clients can put on the table, even if they are not able to offer the consultant an increase in revenues. These might include better access to information about the industry, the use of particularly successful projects as references or simply old-fashioned introductions and recommendations. Many clients underestimate how valuable these things are for consultants. Whatever the objectives you agree with your chosen partners, they need to be in place and agreed by all the parties before any co-ordinated relationship building can occur.

Relationship managers

The objective-setting will not happen by itself—somebody has to do it. On the consultant side, this person may already be in place: once your organization has made the transition from 'client' to 'account' in the consultants' eyes, there is likely to be someone with the role of account or relationship manager in the consulting firm. Unfortunately, this role rarely has a counterpart in the client organization or, where it does, it is either given to a committee or to an individual who has too many other things to do. The consequences of this are that your objectives do not get the consideration they deserve and the consultants' relationship manager quickly falls into a sales management and co-ordination role. They needn't. If you choose to use the relationship manager as your 'champion' within the consulting firm, give him a counterpart to talk to and give him the access he needs, he will be able to perform his role far more effectively and support your organization at most stages of the consulting process and in co-ordinating the overall service portfolio.

Of course, not all relationship managers are created equal and the role will also vary between consulting firms, so you should not necessarily just accept what they offer you. Give some thought to the profile of relationship manager you would like to have from the consulting firm and what you want them to do for you. If you are not happy with the relationship manager that has been allocated to you, say so. Be reasonable in your expectations, though: if you are a relatively small client for the consulting firm, do not expect to get their CEO as a relationship manager; and, if you do, you should not be surprised if they do not spend much time with you. Actually, provided they are senior enough to have a good network in the consulting firm and astute enough to understand your needs, you may well be better off with someone who has the time to actually do some work for you and whose reputation is tied to how well he does this job. If there are any issues, you always have the option to escalate matters to more senior managers.

For this to work well, though, there should also be a client-side relationship manager who can act as a primary point of contact for the consultant. You should design this role based on your needs, but some of the elements you might consider including are:

- to keep sight of all the consulting firm's activities in your organization (e.g. by sitting on steering groups or getting feedback from project managers/directors)
- to provide feedback to the consulting firm through the relevant contacts
- to maintain a direct relationship with a number of key people in the consulting firm
- to facilitate communications between your organization and the consulting firm (by putting people in touch with each other)

- to troubleshoot and arbitrate issues and disputes between
your organization and the consulting firm as they arise
- to keep up-to-date on the people coming and going in
the consulting firm and any changes and developments
in its service offering
- to liaise with the portfolio manager (where applicable) to
identify ways to apply the consultant's service offering to
your requirements
- to work with the consultant relationship manager in
monitoring and managing all aspects of the relationship

I do not see this as a dedicated role (you may disagree) because I
think that the client-side relationship manager should be directly
involved in the activities of your organization and should be sufficiently senior to be able to step in and manage disagreements
when they occur. In view of this and also in view of the fact that
there is quite a lot to do here, it is probably best not to give a single individual too many consulting firms to deal with.

It is important to remember when establishing the relationship manager roles(on both sides) that their role is to manage the
relationship between the organizations and not to be a substitute
for it or a personification of it. Of course, they have to manage
their own relationship, but they also have to ensure that they
know the other organization intimately in their own right (not
just through their opposite number) and to structure and co-ordinate all the individual relationships of which the organizational
relationship is composed.

Relationship design

Once your relationship manager has been in place long enough to
learn their role and you have agreed common goals, the next step
is to 'design' the relationship. This is not quite as contrived and

artificial as it sounds: it involves working back from the agreed objectives and establishing how the relationship must be structured for these goals to be achieved. The key elements in this are:

- Breadth—the number of people, departments or business units involved
- Depth—how well people are expected to know each other, how much time they are likely to spend together and what level of interaction is envisaged
- Information sharing and communication
- Points of contact
- Organizational structures, roles and responsibilities (working groups, relationship teams etc.)
- Joint activities

The last point is probably the most important: without a clear set of activities for the relationship to focus on, the whole exercise can quickly become a talking shop and a waste of everybody's time.

At this point there are two common mistakes which you should aim to avoid: trying to move the relationship from where it is now to where you want it to be in one big step; and expecting that, once the relationship has been planned out and agreed, it will just happen.

The relationship design process has given you an idea of where you want to get to, but to get there you need to have an idea of where you are starting from. In this case, this means understanding the current state of the relationship between the organizations. Again, I should stress that this is not the same thing as the relationship between the individuals who are managing, planning or setting up the relationship. The current relationships between individuals, the skills in place and the level of knowledge about the consulting organization should be assessed with a good dose of honesty and realism. You can then go through a planning process to establish the stages you will need to go through to get from the current state to the desired one, what needs to be done to move from one stage to the next and who should do it.

The 'project' to build the relationship differs somewhat from a project to build a new factory or computer system because the main building blocks are the relationships that exist and develop between individuals. These fluctuate unpredictably and take time to develop. So it is important to give them this time and to build plenty of flexibility into the relationship structure.

Measurement

Where relationship building does not differ from other projects is in managing the benefits. It is often assumed that the benefits of relationships are largely intangible and cannot be measured and tracked. It is true that they are not easy to track, but this does not mean you should not try—and you can be sure that the consultants on the other side of the relationship will be doing their sums very carefully indeed. If you do not monitor the relationship, it can quickly lose its focus and become unproductive. Worse still, there is a danger that the relationship-building activities will snowball and begin to take up too much of the organization's time.

If the objectives set out at the start of the relationship are well thought through, it should be possible to measure (or at least to assess) progress towards them, even if some creativity is required in designing the tracking. For instance, if one of the objectives is to speed up and improve the quality and frequency of market information flowing from the consulting firm to the client, the speed and frequency with which such information is transmitted is relatively easy to measure and the quality can be assessed by the recipients. Based on this sort of tracking, you can adjust activities to move the organizations closer to their objectives and prevent the escalation of unwanted or unproductive activities.

Trust is nice, but control is better

Building long-term relationships with consultants is not without risks. Consultants are not your friends, however personable the individuals may be, and you can and should expect them to exploit any openings that you give them. Their (I should say 'our') detractors often liken them to parasites—they live off a host and, in this case, the host happens to be your organization.

But by some definitions, parasites are not necessarily bad for the host organism and can even be beneficial. Nature provides many examples of symbiotic relationships in which 'parasites' provide valuable services to the host. The same can be true of consultants. And the consultant-parasites differ markedly from their biological brethren in one key respect: whereas a biological host is limited in its ability to choose which parasites it supports, as a client organization you do have the ability to choose your consultants. This means, quite simply, that you have control. You have the power to pick which consultants (if any) you want to build a relationship with and, to a considerable degree, the form that such a relationship should take. Where one hears stories of organizations being infested with consultants who are adding no value and are generally disliked, I am afraid that it is the fault of the managers in those organizations for not exercising the power that they have.

So it is up to you to decide whether you have the time, patience and discipline to impose some control on consulting relationships and whether this effort is worth the benefits you can expect to get for it. And this is not just a 'yes' or 'no' question.

With consulting relationships, as with all the other elements of the consulting mix, you can choose the degree, scope and intensity with which you pursue them. This is what I call 'configuring the mix', the subject of the next chapter.

CHAPTER 9

Configuring the Mix

I suspect many experienced managers will be sceptical about the feasibility of the approach I propose in this book—it does seem like a lot of effort just to improve how you work with consultants. I am not, however, advocating that you take everything I have described in the preceding pages and implement it wholesale. In fact, I would be the first to say that such an approach would be too complex, too disruptive, would require too many resources to bring a return on investment and might ultimately prove unmanageable.

At the end of Chapter 4, I introduced the 'consulting mix' and its four main components: Knowledge management, Learning, Portfolio management and Relationship management. I also mentioned that these components would have to be appropriately balanced to suit your organization. The subsequent chapters described each component, why it is important, what is involved and how it can be achieved independently of the others. Now it is time to circle back and look at how the mix can be configured to suit your organization.

What do I mean by 'configuring the mix'? A culinary analogy might be helpful here: the components of the mix are like ingredients in a recipe. We have looked at how to prepare each ingredient individually, but if your approach to using consultants is to be effective, you need to combine them in the right quantities, in the right sequence and 'cook' them for the right length of time.

The way the components of the mix are applied will differ radically from one organization to another. For instance, an organization aiming to reduce consulting costs in the short term might try to combine co-ordination of consulting activities with better information and controls on the operational aspects of these activities. It would not need to spend much time on relationship management or learning. If the cost reduction objective is extended to the longer term, however, learning will increase in importance because they will need to develop the competencies to keep consulting costs down. On the other hand, an organization wishing to improve a consistently poor track record of implementing consulting projects would do well to focus on learning in order to improve its receptiveness. Or again, if flexibility is the goal, then the emphasis must be placed on relationship and knowledge management.

This process of deciding which components are key and what you need to achieve in each area is what I call 'configuration'. The objective is to take you from a complex scenario in which you have multiple options and conflicting priorities to a clear understanding of what your organization can and should do to improve how it works with consultants.

Timing and factors affecting configuration

It should be clear from the above that the configuration process is essentially about choosing options and making the associated trade-offs. The point at which you move from information gathering and analysis to configuration will depend on preferences and organizational specifics, as will the factors that will influence this configuration. On the question of timing, the only suggestion I would make is that sooner is better than later, if only because information gathering that is not designed to support specific decisions is wasteful of resources.

My approach to the configuration question is similar to the way I suggested you approach knowledge management: I do not have a ready-made solution but prefer instead to take you through the factors you should consider in formulating your own. There are a number of factors to consider and each will tend to pull you in a particular direction. I have discussed most of them earlier in the book, but it is worth pulling them together here so they are in one place.

- *Consulting objectives*—the objectives that you set your-self at the outset are central to framing your approach to consulting. This may sound obvious, but it is surprising how often people loose sight of these during the deci-sion-making process as new and interesting opportuni-ties present themselves. When this happens, the result is usually a loose-knit group of initiatives that are very dif-ficult to bring to a conclusion because the organization's energies have been diluted. Whether the objectives are narrow (ensuring the success of a single, key project) or broad (changing the ratio between internal and external resources in the organization), there should be an inten-sive focus on achieving them first. Anything else may be 'nice to have', but should be considered only after the objectives have been achieved.
- *Competitive environment and organizational development goals*—your consulting objectives are formed within the context of your broader strategy. Their place in this strategy and their importance to it (high or low) will affect the extent and urgency of the transformation and

the resources available for it. Equally, your vision of the future size and shape of your organization and the resourcing strategy that goes with this should give you an idea of the role that consulting is likely to play.

- *Existing competencies*—you will have had to do an initial assessment of how good you are at working with consultants as part of your objective-setting process. But this is not the same as the process of defining what needs to be done to achieve these objectives. So it is worth taking another look at your assessment of where you are now to get a clear picture of the gap that needs to be closed.

- *Structure of your consulting portfolio*—the type of consulting that you use (or are likely to use) and the consequent level of interaction with different parts of your organization will have a major impact on the configuration. For instance, if the consulting is hands-on and operationally focused, there will be a much greater emphasis on learning than if most of the consulting is strategic or market-oriented.

- *Organizational profile and experience of consulting*—the type of people working in your organization (in terms of education, skills, specialization etc.), the experience they have of dealing with consultants (both in terms of the overall exposure and the types of consulting they have been exposed to) and how these people are distributed in the organization will all affect the way different parts of the organization interact with different types of consultant. This in turn will influence both your consultant selection (relationship choices) and your knowledge management.

- *Organizational structure and dynamics*—organizational hierarchies and the decision-making dynamics that take place within them influence the extent to which co-ordination will be needed—or at least the form it is likely to take and the effort needed to put it in place. Where an organization has very dispersed decision-making (by geography, function or business unit), high levels of budgetary autonomy, or a very broad range of consulting requirements, co-ordination and knowledge management become at once more difficult and (usually) more necessary.

- *Culture*—it is hard to overstate the importance of culture in how you approach consulting. It affects how your organization responds to consultants (how receptive it is) at every level. Consultants who work regularly for an organization, have a relationship with it and understand its culture are at a distinct advantage to those who do not, both in terms of selling their work and delivering value. It helps to look at culture from three different perspectives: organizational culture, consulting culture (i.e. attitudes to consulting) and local culture (especially for multinational organizations). In assessing this, you should take care to reflect the realities on the ground and not (as often happens) management's view of what it should be like. Once you have a clear view of how culture is likely to influence receptiveness to consulting, and assuming that you want to improve this, you have two options: change the culture or only select consultants (and consulting projects) that fit this culture. The first takes time and effort and may have consequences (good or bad) that go well beyond the organization's use of consultants; the second can severely limit your room for manoeuvre. So you need to find the right balance between them and also to develop an idea of how this balance is likely to change over time.

• *Feasibility*—an important consideration in deciding what to do is your ability to do it. But the feasibility question should be treated with some caution because it is always easy to find reasons not to do something or to get bogged down in the details of implementation. At the configuration stage, feasibility is not black and white: unless your intentions are grossly out of line with your resources and other constraints, most things are feasible (albeit with a little adjustment and compromise). The focus of configuration is what to do, not how to do it and it is probably best to avoid the temptation to descend into implementation planning (the 'how') until there is some consensus on what is to be implemented.

Approaches to configuration

There are two main approaches to configuring the consulting mix: a 'capability-driven approach' and a 'goal-driven approach'. The first seeks to build on the organization's existing strengths and is essentially incremental in outlook. The second approach is aspirational—you define a future state to which you aspire and then work out how it can be achieved.

Neither of these approaches is inherently better than the other. The goal-driven approach is more comprehensive, but the capability-driven approach is, in many cases, the best way of building value quickly. Each must be judged on its own merits and in the context of the issues the organization faces.

Nor are the two approaches mutually exclusive: it is entirely possible to begin with a capability-driven approach in order to raise your game and, once this is achieved, move on to the more thorough, goal-driven approach. The thing to watch out for in using both approaches is to prevent them from blending too much: in implementing the capability-driven approach, there can be a tendency to gradually make it more and more inclusive, until it begins to resemble the other approach, but without the framework, trade-offs and overall direction that the goal-based approach provides. Equally, a goal-driven approach is likely to be too constrained if you place undue emphasis on quick wins and low-cost options.

The capability-driven approach

Identifying areas for improvement

The capability-based approach begins with the identification of key points of strength and weakness in the organization's use of consultants across the consulting mix (basically a SWOT analysis). Some strengths and weaknesses may not be directly related to consulting (for instance, you may have capabilities that you currently do not apply to consulting that could be applied to this area), so you should aim to be fairly inclusive in carrying out your assessment. This need not be a detailed review, but a quick assessment based on management's views of where past projects have gone wrong, where they feel there is unexploited potential and where the areas of frustration lie. From this you can hypothesize the causes of these weaknesses, the strengths that are underexploited and thus the potential areas to work on.

Selecting and prioritizing

The main criterion in deciding which of these areas to address should be short-term return on investment—you should select those areas where the greatest gains can be made for the least effort and in the shortest time. If this seems like a short-sighted way to address the problem, that is because it is. The capability-based approach is all about making the most of what you have. If you have longer-term objectives and you have chosen to adopt this approach, you have to accept that it is unlikely to be the most efficient or direct route to achieving those objectives. If you try to reconcile the two and avoid any trade-offs, you are likely to end up with a confusing mess in which little or nothing is actually achieved.

The greatest benefits do not always result from the biggest changes. So it is worth keeping an eye out for 'catalytic' changes. In one case I remember, we introduced a weekly phone call between a senior executive of the client organization and the relationship manager of the consulting firm. This was only a ten minute call, but it transformed the relationship because it ensured that both of these senior managers shared an overview of the relationship and were able to identify and head off issues as they arose. It also meant that the people below them started talking to each other more because the questions that came down from the top were no longer phrased in 'them and us' terms and could only be answered through a joint effort. There are often opportunities for such small, high-value changes in the consulting area. Finding them is not always easy, however, because the cause and effect are not often as simple as in the example above. The most effective catalytic changes set off chains of effects that can be far-reaching but hard to predict. So developing your ability to predict and influence these chains is the key to identifying and exploiting this type of opportunity.

Lastly, in view of the emphasis on speed and ease of implementation in this approach, existing organizational constraints should feature in your selection process (which they should not in the objective-driven approach). For instance, there may be a cap on the resources which the organization is prepared to allocate to consulting, regardless of potential benefits; there may be 'no go areas' resulting from other, higher priority activities, from change fatigue or from the risk of conflict with other initiatives; and there may be specific time windows into which these activities have to fit.

Combining and packaging

The selection process should yield a handful of measures that have high potential value and can be implemented with relative ease. These measures may be focused on one area or spread across the consulting mix. So far you will probably have been looking at them independently. In practice, though, they are unlikely to be independent of each other, either in terms of their implementation or their effects, and you will need to package the measures so that costs can be shared, the benefits reinforce each other and the implementation sequence makes optimal use of resources and fits with other things that are going on in your organization. If you do not, you could find that you are duplicating your implementation efforts and costs, that your measures cancel each other out and that implementation is tricky and expensive.

While the capability-driven approach lays more emphasis on selection and speed than on this combination and packaging of measures (which is key to the objectives-based approach), there can still be quite a bit of value in getting the combination right.

The strengths of the capability-driven configuration process are that it is quick, cost effective and avoids complexity. It generally suits organizations for which the benefits from better use of consultants are limited, those who do not have the time, available resources or the appetite to carry out a more comprehensive process, or those for whom a highly dynamic environment precludes a longer term approach. The corresponding weaknesses of the process are that it has a relatively short-term focus, it can compound imbalances in the organization's capabilities, it does not exploit the full potential that could be achieved and it avoids complexity rather than addressing it.

The goal-driven approach

This approach to configuring the consulting mix requires a good deal more effort than the capability-driven approach. The benefits are also (usually) more substantial, albeit longer term. So it should be viewed as an investment over a multi-year timescale. Like any such investment it is worth taking the time to build a strong consensus on benefits and senior-level commitment to drive the project through.

Strategy and objectives

The starting point of this process is a view of consultants as an asset within the organization's broader strategic armoury and the organization's ability to work with consultants as the mechanism for exploiting this asset. In other words, consultants are viewed as an integral element in the organization's resourcing and organizational development strategies. This does not mean that the intention is to use consultants more (it may be the opposite), but that you take an integrated and balanced view of how you use them.

The process kicks off with a cascade of objectives (which is less dramatic than it sounds). Starting with the organization's strategic objectives, you look at how consultants can be used to further these objectives. This can then be fleshed out into a view of the role consultants will play as your organization develops. This role definition can in turn form the basis for your medium-term consulting objectives.

Designing a coherent system

Once you know where you want to go, you can look at what you need to get there: the competencies and capabilities that you need to put in place for your objectives to be achieved. Unlike with the capability-driven approach, you are not selecting measures for their ease of implementation here, but for the coherence that they bring to your overall programme. You are not simply making improvements, but trying to build a system (structures, processes, people and culture) that is self-sustaining, self- optimizing and, if you get it right, constantly improving. So you will need to spend a considerable amount of time looking not only at how the measures you plan to take will affect your organization, but also how they will affect each other over time. This is a complex process, with many variables and sensitivities that are not easy to identify, let alone predict. You will at times get it wrong. But hopefully the process of working through these dynamics and the understanding you have developed in doing this, will have prepared you to deal with the inevitable occasions when things do not work out as you had intended.

Understanding the challenge

It is only at the point when you have a fairly comprehensive and detailed view of what you are trying to achieve and how it will work that you should bring your intentions face to face with the realities on the ground: the objectives and deliverables you have defined must be set against your analysis of where you are today. This gap analysis will yield two results: an idea of the effort required to achieve your objectives, both in terms of level and focus; and an understanding of the complexities, issues and trade-offs that will need to be resolved before you can begin organizing the tasks into projects that can be implemented.

Again, the time and effort required to resolve the issues that emerge from the gap analysis should not be underestimated. Equally, the value of this effort should not be overlooked: it can make the difference between a successful implementation that has a transformative effect on your organization and one that is, at best, a modest improvement on where you are now. How you do this is a matter of style and preference. My own approach is to try to map out the constraints, trade-offs, dependencies and links and distil all of this into a set of decisions. I then look at the relative importance of these decisions and when they need to be made, grouping them into those that fall before implementation and those that can be resolved during implementation. The more decisions that fall before implementation, the easier it will be to plan and the less flexibility there will be once implementation has started.

The strengths of the goal-driven approach are that it is comprehensive and leads to a robust structure for the consultant management initiative that is aligned with the organization's strategic goals while taking adequate account of existing assets and constraints. Unlike the capability-driven approach, it seeks to remedy the organization's weaknesses as well as leveraging its strengths and it addresses the complexities that emerge head-on rather than avoiding them.

The weaknesses of the approach are that it is more expensive than the capability-driven approach, has relatively long timescales and, as a consequence of this, can prove unwieldy in a constantly changing environment.

Implementing your consulting mix

The details of implementation and implementation planning fall outside the scope of this book: they are likely to be highly specific to the organization in which they are to be enacted and to the consulting mix that has been configured for it. Success will depend on the effective application of generic programme management disciplines and experience. There are, however, a few things I would like to point out that I think are particularly relevant to implementing a structured approach to consulting.

First (and foremost) is the question of *senior-level sponsorship*. In the introduction to this book I looked at some of the reasons why so few organizations attempt to improve the way they use consultants. High on this list was the general apathy towards consulting that resulted from a view that it is peripheral or unimportant. If it is genuinely unimportant, then you do not need to be doing anything about it. On the other hand, if your analysis has determined that it is important and you have decided to do something about it, then it is incumbent on senior management to provide a counterbalance to the general indifference that you are likely to encounter elsewhere in the organization. And this level of support must be sustained throughout the change programme.

For similar reasons to the above, someone must assume *leadership and responsibility* for the overall programme. This person may or may not eventually become the consulting portfolio manager (there are some obvious advantages to this), but they have to be sufficiently senior to command the attention of all those who will be directly affected by the project.

The third area that merits some careful attention is *timing*. In most projects there is a heavy emphasis on deadlines and cramming as much as possible into a limited time-frame. I would advise caution if you are planning on doing this here because it can be counter-productive. Where the objectives you set involve changes in the way the organization works, it will take time for these changes to bed down. If the changes are to stick, it is essential to allow time for any wrinkles to be ironed out, for reinforcement, and simply for people to get used to them.

Lastly, look to the *ancillary benefits*. Each element in the mix has the potential to benefit the organization beyond the more efficient and effective use of consultants (for those of you skipping ahead, I have tried to point some of these out in the preceding chapters). It may well be that these benefits are greater than those to be achieved in the consulting area alone. In some cases, achieving these ancillary benefits will involve considerable additional effort. In others, it won't. It would be a shame to let such opportunities go by unexploited, or without at least having considered exploiting them. This works both ways: there may be other projects in the organization which could (again with very little effort) contribute to the implementation of the consulting mix. It is worth keeping an eye out for these and using them where it is appropriate.

CHAPTER 10

A Strategic Perspective

Much of this book has been concerned with the practicalities of improving how an organization works with consultants. Rolling up your sleeves and getting down to the nitty-gritty is essential if you are to make progress in this area. But in focusing on the practicalities, it is easy to lose sight of the end point. How far could you go with the suggestions in this book? What could your organization look like once you have implemented the changes? How does this differ from the organization you have today? And what opportunities does this present?

In this chapter I will try to answer these questions by describing how the consulting relationship could look if all the suggestions in this book are applied and then suggesting some of the strategic opportunities that arise.

The effective client

The description that follows is my attempt to show how the consulting relationship could work and how all the elements discussed in this book tie together to make your organization an effective user of consultants. I am conscious that few organizations, even with the best will in the world and the greatest of efforts, will be able to achieve everything that is set out here—reality has a way of curbing our aspirations. I feel it is important, however, to have an idea of what these aspirations could be if they are to be even partially achieved.

So what happens when an organization decides to get better at working with consultants?

On the most basic level, there is a much higher awareness in the organization of the role that consultants (and other external suppliers) play, of the issues involved and of how to facilitate this by being a 'good client'. Being a good client greatly enhances the value for money of consulting projects because the projects are well-defined, well-structured and well-managed, the right consultants are selected to carry them out and because the right environment has been created for them to be successful. The perception of value for money is also higher because of effective benefits measurement and management and because the portfolio of consulting projects is managed and co-ordinated to avoid duplication and waste.

This perception of value for money, combined with better awareness, better information and the sense of control which results from good co-ordination and strong relationships, leads to much greater confidence in using consultants. The organization becomes at once more assertive and less antagonistic when dealing with its consulting suppliers.

This in turn leads to much greater collaboration between the organization and its consultants and this collaboration goes well beyond set-piece consulting projects. The consultants' information resources are available for the organization's employees to use. Where before, employees used their colleagues as sounding boards for new ideas and initiatives, they now also use their contacts within consulting firms. The consultants, for their part, use the relationship as a sounding board for their own service development and the client helps the consultants market these services by publicising success stories and by referring the consultants to their business partners.

As trust, confidence and collaboration develop, the organization gradually begins to let go of the urge to be good at everything and to have control over all aspects of its activities. This is a difficult habit to break because it is driven by people's insecurities, but once people see that third parties can carry out the activities that they are less good at and do them better, and once this impression has been reinforced by experience, the barriers begin to come down. This has important implications for the way the organization works because it allows it to focus on and understand its core competencies and processes and so develop its competitive advantages.

The doctrine of core competencies has, of course, been around for many years and is a staple of strategy papers. Unfortunately, all too often it remains at the strategic level—an expression of management's desires rather than an operational reality. This high-level thinking may help set direction, but it is not the same as a grass roots understanding of what your organization is good at and bad at, and how good or bad it is relative to others. This type of understanding is a necessary precondition to effective development of these competencies.

All this adds up to a change in the organization's attitudes and culture. Consultants may (occasionally) still be regarded as parasites, but as parasites that can be good for the organization and on whom the organization depends—the relationship becomes symbiotic. This attitude is extended to other service providers and the organization becomes more open and less self-reliant.

Further opportunities?

For most organizations the road to achieving the state I have just described is likely to be fairly long. And when you get there, you have good reason to be satisfied. But the road does not need to end at this point. In achieving these goals, you have built up new capabilities and competencies in knowledge management, co-ordination and relationship management. Your organization will also have become better at learning both incrementally and by absorbing new concepts and techniques. These competencies and capabilities are assets which the organization can exploit well beyond the initial objective of using consultants better. And the change in organizational culture which has occurred in parallel with this competency development means that the organization is ready to exploit them.

So what are the opportunities and how can you make the most of them? The most obvious opportunity is to extend the operating mode you have developed with your consultants at both ends of the supply chain to include other suppliers on the one hand and customers on the other (although the extent to which customers can be included will depend on the type of activity and customer).

This 'vertical' collaboration can be extended horizontally to include other organizations in different industries or areas of activity. Why would you want to collaborate with unrelated organizations? Because you can learn from each other's experience and pool resources: the vast majority of processes, skills and capabilities are common to many organizations (hence the common accusation of 'cookie-cutter consulting'). As a consultant, I have occasionally brought managers from one client to see another and discuss a project that I have carried out with them. Without exception, both sides have said it was extremely useful.

It could be far more useful if it was done regularly and systematically. Again, this cross-fertilization of ideas and issues is not uncommon at the top of an organization (board members, for instance, commonly have advisory roles for several organizations), but it is rare to see it fully exploited and even rarer to see it happening further down the organization where it can have a more immediate and practical impact.

Once you have established yourself as a collaborative organization, you can consider extending the model further to become a 'networked' organization. The 'networked organization' was something of a buzzword in the late 1990s. To be credible, everyone was in pursuit of 'network effects' as part of a 'new paradigm'. Not all of this is hokum. Few people in business or government would deny the benefits of effective and well-organized personal networking. There is no reason why the same should not apply at the organizational level. But it must be 'effective' and 'well organized' and this is where much of the organizational networking of the 1990s fell down: networking was pursued as an end in itself without much thought to how it could be exploited or where it would create value and without the capabilities in place to make it succeed. Networking and collaboration were often lumped together in people's minds or it was assumed that networking would automatically lead to collaboration. The result in many cases was that organizations that were relatively unstable in themselves, and that had little or no experience of organizational collaboration, expended considerable effort in developing a broad and fundamentally shallow network which provided little in the way of economic benefit and dissipated the organizations' energies.

The networking we are considering here comes at a later stage in the organization's development, where sufficient capabilities are in place to avoid most of the pitfalls mentioned above. Even so, if you plan to put effort and resources into organizational networking, it is important not to stumble into it in a haphazard manner: you need clarity of objectives and means. The objectives are up to you to decide. As for the means, you have a major asset that you can exploit to facilitate your networking—the relationship you have built with your consultants. Consultants are ideally placed to act as brokers for organizational networks: they manage extensive networks themselves; they are constantly exposed to the issues faced by the organizations in these networks and so can assess where common issues or common interests exist; and they are, broadly speaking and in this context, impartial third parties. Unfortunately, most consultancies have not been as active as they could have been in performing this role on their clients' behalf— largely because of indifference or lack of initiative on the client side. But the opportunity remains there for the taking, if a client is prepared to show the drive and commitment to exploit it alongside their consultants.

There are those who will say that, if their goal was to achieve an open, collaborative, networked organization, they would not start by looking at consulting. Indeed, the management of consultants may seem a very roundabout route to achieving it. And I would be the first to agree that there are many ways to achieving these goals depending on the situation in which your organization finds itself. But I would also argue that an approach through consulting offers some distinct advantages: the consulting relationship I described earlier is complex in ways that most supplier relationships are not and if you can build the capabilities to manage consulting relationships effectively, the management of other relationships should be relatively easy by comparison. The level of commitment and consequently the risk is considerably lower if you take the consulting route—trying to change your relationship with key suppliers can lead to horrific repercussions if it goes wrong, whereas, if a consulting relationship goes wrong, the damage is relatively short term. Lastly, as I said above, consultants are an ideal linchpin for the organizational communities envisaged here. For these reasons, I would argue that the consulting route is at least as likely to succeed as other approaches, though it is also likely to be slower and more painstaking.

Making it happen

I hope this chapter has made you more aware of the opportunities that can present themselves when you build the capabilities needed to work with consultants. Even if your ambitions do not extend as far as what I have outlined in here, it should be clear that there is significant potential. And yet, despite the increasing pressure to find efficiency and productivity improvements in modern organizations (not just commercial ones), this potential remains largely untapped. To me, this indicates that there are considerable barriers to overcome if you are to get at the value. I discussed many of these barriers during the course of the book: attitudes towards consultants and the role of consulting, organizational culture, entrenched habits, the fact that consulting has historically been a marginal activity and, perhaps most importantly, the lack of awareness that stems from the fact that consulting activities tend to be dispersed throughout an organization. And commercial imperatives mean that the consultants rarely make any attempt to change the game.

The upshot of all this is that the way most clients work with consultants has been stuck in a rut for the last three decades (the exception being the emergence of outsourcing and partnership deals which, to my mind, go beyond the scope of consulting) and consultant-client relationships are often mildly antagonistic and frustrating for both sides. The challenge for anyone wishing to implement the suggestions in this book is how to build sufficient momentum to overcome the barriers and the organizational inertia, and bring about a lasting change.

The answer to this question is as simple as it is important: do something! I do not mean go and do some analysis. I mean pick the three or four actions you feel would make the most difference for your organization (you probably already know what they are) and implement them. The only way to build awareness and momentum for change is to actually start making the change happen. With luck and persistence, you will be able to push things to a point where the change becomes self-perpetuating, but even if you do not, you will have developed capabilities you did not have before and created some value in the process.

The benefits these capabilities bring need not be limited to the organizations that develop them. If they are adopted widely enough, they have the potential to transform the industry because the more clients make these initial changes, the more consultants are likely to respond and adapt to the new way of doing things. The more change there is, the more there will be, because it will make it easier for more organizations to join in and for those that have already started to develop their capabilities further. The eventual result will, I hope, be a more effective consulting industry serving more capable clients to the benefit of all involved.

Index

Index